EDITOR: MARTIN WIN

 OSPREY
MILITARY

ELITE SER

ATTILA AND THE NOMAD HORDES

Text by
DAVID NICOLLE PHD
Colour plates by
ANGUS McBRIDE

Published in 1990 by
Osprey Publishing Ltd
59 Grosvenor Street, London W1X 9DA
© Copyright 1990 Osprey Publishing Ltd
Reprinted 1992

British Library Cataloguing in Publication Data
Nicolle, David, *1944–*
  Attila and the nomad hordes.—(Elite series; no.30).
  1. Asia. Inner Asia. Nomadic tribes, history
  I. Title   II. Series
  951
ISBN 0 85045 996 6
21873658
Filmset in Great Britain
Printed through Bookbuilders Ltd, Hong Kong

Dedication: In memoriam Eugen & Anthea Heer

Artist's Note
Readers may care to note that the original paintings
from which the colour plates in this book were
prepared are available for private sale. All
reproduction copyright whatsoever is retained by the
publisher. All enquiries should be addressed to:
  Scorpio Gallery,
  P.O. Box 475,
  Hailsham,
  E. Sussex BN27 2SL
The publishers regret that they can enter into no
correspondence upon this matter.

Attila and the Nomad Hordes

Introduction

Of all the conquerors who swept out of Central Asia, two names stand out in European memory— Attila the Hun and Genghis Khan the Mongol. Both are remembered for massacres and devastation; yet whereas Genghis is also famous for the laws he imposed on half of Asia and for the trade which flourished under Mongol rule, Attila's notoriety seems unrelieved by positive achievements. But what was Attila's short-lived empire really like? What happened to the Huns afterwards, and what rôle did the nomads of Central Asia play in the centuries between Attila and Genghis Khan?

During the murky years before Attila's reign the Huns may have jostled the Goths, Vandals and other Germanics into the so-called Great Migrations, which in turn eventually destroyed half the Roman Empire. Around AD 445 Attila won the leadership of a confederacy of tribes and from then on the Huns grew from a barbarian nuisance into a deadly peril for the Romans. In 451, however, Attila's invasion of northern France ended in defeat, and two years later he died. His empire was divided between quarrelling sons and collapsed almost without trace. Yet from this unpromising record arose legends which made Attila the Hun into one of the fiercest ogres of European history.

Attila did use theatrical rages to inspire fear, while his campaigns show ruthlessness as well as strategic skill. Like Genghis Khan, Attila clung to the simple life of his ancestors despite vast wealth. Like Genghis he frequently preferred political manoeuvre to open battle and, despite the reports of Roman and Greek chroniclers, was no mere savage. Nor was he a 'divine ruler' to his own tribesmen, merely a great warrior-leader who, on his death, was buried with simple Turco-Mongol ceremony. The Huns also had their own culture which, though alien to the Classical world, was

The serpent beneath a Roman Emperor's foot on this gold coin may be the only contemporary 'portrait' of Attila. Minted under the co-Emperors Valentinian III and Marcian, it is believed to commemorate Roman victories over the Huns. (British Mus., C.191BT.9, London)

neither barbarous nor any more cruel than that of the Roman Empire. Attila's greatest crime was to be different, in physical appearance, cultural background and attitude towards urban civilisation. Even these differences seem to have been exaggerated, for by the time Attila built his empire the Huns were no longer simply steppe nomads.

It was Attila's foes who raised him to the status of an alien monster. Roman coins portrayed the Huns as a demonic human-headed serpent—the ancient symbol of those irrational giants who once fought Zeus. Other monuments to the defeat of the feared Hun might be a series of crude Roman carvings in eastern France. Yet the greatest memorial must be Attila's rôle as the wicked Etzel in the medieval German epic poem *The Nibelungenlied* which inspired Wagner's overblown operatic cycle of *The Ring*.

Chronology[1]

[1] See also MAA 105 *The Mongols*, MAA 125 *The Armies of Islam 7th–11th Centuries*, MAA 171 *Saladin and the Saracens*, MAA 175 *Rome's Enemies (3): Parthians and Sassanid Persians*, MAA 195 *Hungary and the fall of Eastern Europe 1000–1568* and Elite 19 *The Crusades*.

(Central Asian peoples shown in *italics*)

220 Fall of Chinese Han dynasty; China under fragmented local dynasties.

304–15 *Hsiung-nu* invade China.

330 Capital of Roman Empire moved to Constantinople (Istanbul).

c.350 *Huns* invade Iran and India.

c.370 *'Black' Huns* overrun *Alans* north of Black Sea.

402–10 Unification of *Juan-Juan* along north Chinese frontier.

443–47 *'Black' Huns* invade Thrace and Greece.

445 Attila becomes sole ruler of *'Black' Huns*.

447 *'Black' Huns* cross Danube, invade Eastern Roman Empire.

451 Defeat of Attila by Western Romans and allies at battle of Catalaunian Fields.

453 Death of Attila, collapse of *'Black' Hun* Empire in Europe.

476 End of Western Roman Empire.

480 *Hephthalite 'White Huns'* destroy Gupta Empire of India.

484 *Hephthalite 'White Huns'* kill Sassanian Emperor of Iran.

552 Establishment of *Gök 'Blue' Turkish* state in Central Asia.

558–70 *Avars* enter Europe, establish state in Hungary.

571 *Gök 'Blue' Turks* and Sassanian Iranians destroy *Hephthalite 'White' Hun* state and divide Transoxania–eastern Iran between them.

c.585 *Gök 'Blue' Turkish* state divided into *Eastern Turkish* and *Western Turkish* Khanates.

601 *Avars* defeated by Byzantines (Eastern Romans).

618 Sui dynasty overthrown by T'ang dynasty in China.

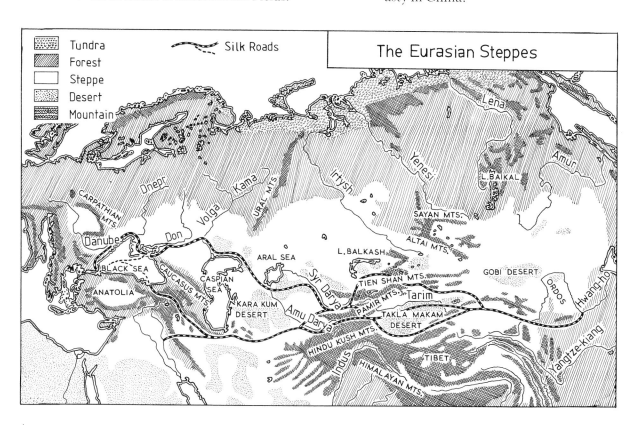

Carved funeral couch from northern China (northern Ch'i dynasty AD 550–557). One rider wears a Central Asian coat and has a long straight sword while a Turkish tassel hangs from his bridle. He does not yet use stirrups. Another scene shows a large dagger in a flared sheath. Identical weapons appeared wherever Central Asian Turkic peoples ruled. (Mus. of Fine Arts, inv. 12.588–9, Boston)

626	*Avar*-Sassanian alliance besieges Constantinople.
636–51	Muslim Arabs conquer Sassanian Iran.
658	Chinese power reaches greatest extent in Central Asia.
665	Tibetans expand into Central Asia.
679	*Bulgars* cross Danube, found state of Bulgaria.
739	Consolidation of Arab Muslim power in Transoxania.
744	Destruction of *Eastern Turkish* Khanate.
745	Establishment of *Uighur* Empire in Central Asia.
751	Muslim Arabs defeat T'ang Chinese at battle of Talas.
763	Collapse of T'ang Chinese authority in Central Asia.
803	Collapse of *Avar* state in Central Europe.
811	*Bulgars* defeat Byzantines at Adrianople (Edirne).
840	*Uighur* Empire overthrown by *Kirghiz*.
840–42	Collapse of central authority in Tibet, disintegration of Tibetan Empire in Central Asia.
865	*Bulgarians* and Serbians converted to Christianity.
899	*Magyars* cross Carpathians into Hungary.
907–960	China fragmented under 'Five Dynasties'.
915	First *Pecheneg* raids into Russia.
916	Foundation of *Khitai* state in Mongolia.
922	Unification of *Volga Bulgars*.
947	*Khitai* overrun northern China.
955	*Magyars* defeated by German Empire at battle of Lech.
965–67	Prince Svyatoslav of Kiev breaks power of *Khazar* Empire.

979	China largely reunited under Sung dynasty.
999	Muslim *Karakhanids* seize Transoxania.
1018	Byzantium overthrows first *Bulgarian* kingdom in Balkans.
1036	Major defeat of *Pechenegs* by Russian Prince of Kiev.
1054	Kievan Russia fragments in rival principalities, first major *Kipchaq* raids into Russia.
1091	Byzantines and *Kipchaq* allies defeat *Pechenegs*.
1093	*Kipchaqs* sack Kiev.
1125	Unification of *Kipchaqs* in southern Russia.
1125–26	*Jurchen (Chin)* conquer *Khitai* northern China, *Khitai* migrate westward and establish *Karakhitai* state (c.1140).
c.1165	Muslim *Karakhanids* overthrown by Buddhist *Karakhitai*.
1167	Birth of Genghis Khan.
1206	Start of *Mongol* conquests under Genghis Khan.

The Nomads and their Neighbours

The steppes which once stretched from eastern Romania to the Pacific Ocean were not identical from end to end; climates varied, and they were divided by rivers, hills and deserts. Northward lay the Russian and Siberian forests, and southward other forests, wastes, vast mountain ranges and regions of intensive agriculture. Separated from the main Eurasian steppe lay other broad areas of prairie such as the Hungarian Plain in Europe, various Middle Eastern grasslands, the high steppes of Tibet and, deep in the Siberian forest, the little-known steppes of Angaraland. Forests formed the main frontiers and were always an obstacle to steppe people. Although Turkish tribes did penetrate these woodlands they had to change

their way of life once there. Rivers were more a means of communication than a barrier, while mountains often served as important sources of iron. Almost all nomadic tribes were involved in some agriculture and would only retreat into the deep steppes when forced.

Even within the Eurasian steppe, nomad culture was divided into two bands. The northern belt was the home of the true nomadic tribes, while through the drier southern belt ran the famous Silk Roads, those ancient trading routes which linked China to the Middle East. Settled peoples inhabited the oases along these roads and were strongly influenced by civilizations to the east, south and west. Yet they were also of nomad origin and were generally under the domination of powerful nomadic tribes.

It was the horse which gave the Central Asian nomad his amazing military power. Raised upon the grasslands in enormous numbers, the supply was not, however, inexhaustible. Nor were surplus horses of any value to a nomad except for trade or war. Herein lay the tribes' problem. Steppe life

Guardian carved on a stone 'mortuary house' of AD 527. Made in China under the northern Toba (Wei) dynasty it shows the lamellar armour, rectangular shield and straight single-edged sword used by some Toba infantry. (Mus. of Fine Arts, inv. 37.340, Boston)

meant the dispersal of people and thus of military potential. Conquest meant gathering tribal man-power into an army, while domination over settled civilizations, like those of China and the Middle East, took the nomad away from the steppes which fed his great horse-herds and from the harsh free-ranging life which made him a great warrior.

Nor was a herdsman necessarily a nomad. Nomadic warfare was characterized by great speed across enormous distances, but many Central Asian peoples travelled slowly with their homes and families in cumbersome waggons. The steppes also grew narrower as the tribes moved west, forcing them to change their way of life. Those peoples who, like the Huns, Avars and Magyars, crossed the Carpathian Mountains into the Hungarian Plain found this small prairie unable to support the number of horses needed by a truly nomadic army. If they raided deeper the situation became worse, warrior bands having to scatter in search of pasture and finding it very difficult to regroup in the forests and fields of Europe. The influence of ecology on military history has yet to be properly studied, but it is clear that the Hungarian Plain could never support a nomadic 'superpower'. However important the Huns, Avars and others might seem in European history, they remained minor peoples who had been driven out of the steppes by more successful tribes.

The steppe tribes were not ethnic units, though to European eyes most appeared as typical Turco-Mongol peoples. Tribes evolved, changed, disappeared. Enemy deserters, prisoners or mercenaries

Ruins of a Chinese fort near the Jade Gate, a western entry point into the Chinese Empire. In the heart of Central Asia the frontier was marked by a series of forts, watch-towers and walls forming a frontier zone comparable to the Roman limes. **(Aurel Stein)**

could be drawn in. Loyalty was based both on kinship and on the free choice of comrades. A leader's authority varied depending on outside cultural influence. Among the pre-Islamic Turks a king or *Khagan* could be a semi-divine link between heaven and earth, as in Iran or China. Religious beliefs were even more varied, ranging from tribal shamanism and a belief in a multitude of spirits to a monotheistic belief in one god, 'Tengri of the Blue Sky'. Neighbouring religions also had followers in the steppe, including Buddhism, Manicheism, Zoroastrianism, Judaism, Christianity and Islam. Islam was ultimately victorious and its spread was peaceful, via merchants and missionaries, after the initial Arab conquest of Transoxania. Its inherent democracy also demoted the semi-divine status of many rulers.

The reasons why Central Asian peoples were pushed into migration or war with their neigh-bours varied. Defeat normally meant absorption rather than extermination. On the other hand the military elite of a defeated tribe might migrate rather than be demoted, and could recruit new followers as it went. War was also a way of getting essentials or luxury goods from settled neighbours. Nevertheless warfare was governed by strict rules. Horses had to be well fed, which normally meant campaigning in early autumn. The Turks began most expeditions under a full moon, while the Uighurs avoided war beneath certain stars.

Ruins of an arsenal in the Chinese frontier zone at Tun-Huang. This area formed a strategic corridor linking China with its vassals or allies in Sinkiang. (Aurel Stein)

According to traditions which survive in the form of poetry, individual combat would begin with archery, followed by swords and spears, after which the heroes would disarm and wrestle. Having thus tested each other's worth the heroes would traditionally become friends before setting off in search of further adventure. Parallels with European knights are obvious, particularly where the 'belted warrior' was concerned—a highly decorated weapons-belt mirroring the *cingulam* of the Christian knight. In such cases of similarity the Central Asian fashion almost always came before that seen in the West, and there can be little doubt about the enormous impact that steppe peoples had on military history and military fashion. Small wonder that the 9th century Arab commentator Al Jahiz described the rôle of the Turks in war as being like that of the Greeks in science or the Chinese in art.

Cavalry, archery and speed of manoeuvre rather than numbers made the steppe nomad virtually invincible within his own terrain, at least until the spread of firearms. The tribes were also able to feed and supply to an army huge numbers of horses when needed. On the other hand almost all nomad forces, particularly those of the great empires, employed infantry and either erected or used existing fortifications. Professional infantry served the *Khagan* of the 8th century Gök Turks and of the 9th century Uighurs. The heroes of Turkish epic, unlike proud European knights, had

no objection to fighting on foot, despite the testimony of Western writers who claimed that the Huns and others could hardly walk due to their bandy legs.

Settled civilizations rarely understood the nomads' motives for war. Instead they dwelt on their unpredictable eruptions out of the steppes and, in Western eyes, their frightening appearance. Even today it is rarely realized that relations between nomads and settled peoples were mostly peaceful and that mutually profitable trade was rarely interrupted even in wartime. Some historians still put nomad military successes down to the divisions or decadence of their settled foes, failing to realize that the military potential of the nomad was far greater than that of the peasant or townsman.

While Europe developed a racist contempt for the feared 'Asiatic' nomad, the Chinese remained trapped within their own fiction of Central Asian 'barbarians' providing tribute to the 'Son of Heaven'. In reality the nomads, however backward, reflected the cultures of the settled civilizations from which they borrowed economic, social and even military systems. The barbarian floods which periodically breached the walls of civilization were themselves a product of settled culture, either through the nomads' wish to control what they already admired or in response to 'civilized' aggression into the steppes. Even the settled states' efforts to insulate themselves behind walls or militarized frontier *limes* further stimulated contact through war or trade. Many such frontiers were very blurred—a fact which historical atlases

rarely show—examples being found in the Byzantine Balkans, southern Russia, Muslim Transoxania and western China. Such zones would, in fact, play a major rôle in the spread of settled technology to the nomads and of nomad tactics to the settled states. New political systems, including the earliest forms of feudalism, often emerged in these regions.

Since most history has been written by settled peoples, it is not surprising that nomad aggression has been emphasized, yet there was plenty of settled aggression into the steppes. Barbarian attacks on China often responded to Chinese advances into areas suitable for both nomad pastoralism and for settled agriculture. Even before the Muslim conquest of Transoxania there had been a shift of power away from the nomads. The fertile but drought-prone Black Earth country of southern Russia was suitable for stock-raising and cereal production. Both the Turco-Mongol tribes and the Russian princes coveted this land while the people who lived there tended to keep cattle and to grow crops. The Russian princes also wanted control of the great rivers down to the Black Sea which were rich trade routes to Byzantium and beyond. While Russians built forts and islands of agriculture in a sea of steppe grass, the nomads checked the spread of Slav agriculture by destroying both crops and forts. Fortunes also wavered back and forth on the westernmost fringe of the steppe in Moldavia, with nomads pushing in from the Ukraine and Vlach Romanians filtering down from the Carpathian Mountains. Even in the heart of the steppe around Lake Balkash,

Walls and a watch-tower near the western end of the Chinese frontier zone at Tun-Huang. They are built from layers of reeds and mud in a style which would influence later fortifications in Central Asia. (Aurel Stein)

Painted clay tomb figures of the northern Toba (Wei) dynasty, 5th century northern China. (British Mus., no. 1952.10–28.15, London)

9

Turkish villagers gradually, and with many a setback, pushed back the similarly Turkish nomads.

The generally higher status which merchants enjoyed in Central Asia benefitted their neighbours but helped the nomads to gain a clear picture of the situation beyond their borders. The Chinese,

Iranian and Byzantine habit of enlisting nomad mercenaries also provided Central Asian peoples with accurate intelligence. In general they understood the strengths and weaknesses of their settled neighbours, and knew exactly what they wanted whenever they chose to raid across the frontier.

When part of a tribe migrated, willingly or otherwise, it took its families and livestock along. Settled civilizations were thus faced by a people, not merely an army. In parts of the Balkans and Transoxania this forced the previous inhabitants up into the mountains. Sometimes these earlier peoples drifted back to assimilate rather than reconquer the Turkish nomads. Sometimes the nomads infiltrated the mountain valleys, but they rarely settled the forested slopes. Instead some nomadic peoples provided local leadership or new ruling dynasties, as did the 7th–8th century Bulgars or the 11th and 12th century Kipchaqs in Bulgaria and Wallachia. These rising states were not, however, to be Turkic, for the nomads formed a tiny, and soon assimilated, minority. Even when nomad invaders were defeated they were rarely wiped out or even expelled. In southern Russia, for example, they were settled by the Russian princes as military colonies, defending the settled frontiers against other nomads. The nomads' contribution to history was not merely destructive, for these seemingly alien tribesmen stimulated trade, provided political leadership, and had a profound influence on the development of tactics and military technology in lands as far apart as Western Europe, Byzantium, Russia, Iran and China.

Weapons, Horses, Transport and Fortifications

The peoples of Central Asia learned many military techniques from China, but they also taught much and, in fact, they were the channel through which Chinese military science reached Europe and the

Painted clay tomb figure of around AD 500. This infantryman is an example of the Chinese troops that the nomads employed after they conquered northern China. (British Mus., no. 1925.10–15.1, London)

Middle East. In their own mythology, however, the war god Ch'ih-yo invented archery and all arms and armour. War gods featured prominently in Central Asian shamanism, not only of the Turco-Mongols but also of the Indo-European nomads. The Iranian Alans worshipped a war god in the form of a naked sword thrust into the earth, an idea recalling the British myth of Arthur's Excaliber—'The Sword in the Stone'. The Huns may also have worshipped their war god in the form of a sword, while a large dagger symbolized the war god to many Central Asian peoples, and a sword was central to Turkish oath taking, as it would become to the knights of Christian Europe.

While primitive bone arrowheads and stone axes continued to be used in some areas, the Turks first appeared as the 'blacksmiths' of their Juan-Juan masters and Central Asian metalworkers were invariably respected. Muslims were amazed by the Turkish warrior's apparent ability to make or repair all his own equipment, and archaeology has shown the first Bulgarian capital at Pliska to have had a flourishing armourers' quarter.

Forest peoples to the north accepted the military technology of the steppes, and Central Asia influenced Middle Eastern and Roman weaponry even before the Great Migrations of the 4th and 5th centuries. Thereafter European smiths and armourers learned from the East right up to the 13th century, while Islamic weaponry never ceased to be under Turco-Mongol influence. On the other hand much iron lamellar armour found in the steppes may be of Iranian or Transoxanian origin, Turco-Mongol armourers generally making hardened leather lamellar. Yet this did not mean that the settled governments welcomed an arms trade with the steppes. Chinese authorities tried to stop the export of military hardware to the nomads, as did the Byzantine Empire, though both permitted their own troops to adopt superior 'barbarian' military fashions.

Some archaeologists maintain that almost all weapons found among the nomad-ruled peoples of the medieval Balkans are of Byzantine origin. Competing modern nationalisms cloud this issue, but it is certainly difficult to distinguish Slav, nomad and Byzantine arms during these early centuries. There was a strong Western influence on the weaponry of Eastern Europe even when these

Lamellar helmets appear in early medieval Central Asian art. Here such protection is worn by a clay tomb-figure from the Toba period. His enormous boots suggest that he was a cavalryman. (British Mus., no. 1973.7–26.181, London)

areas were ruled by peoples from the steppes, while further east the weaponry of the once nomadic Volga Bulgars soon became similar to that of their Russian rivals. Meanwhile the Russians not only exported arms but were under persistent military influence from both the steppes and from western Europe. This picture may be confusing, but such

The outlines of lamellar horse-armour can still be seen on another clay tomb figure of the northern Toba (Wei) period. The animal has a chamfron on its head while the angle of the rider's foot suggests that he uses stirrups. (British Mus., no. 1936.10–12.292, London)

an interplay of influences led to sophisticated military technology, often far in advance of that seen in western Europe until the later Middle Ages.

Bows

Of all Central Asian weapons the bow remained paramount. The typical Central Asian type was of composite wood, horn and sinew construction, often with bone stiffeners. It was usually asymmetrical with a characteristically thick bow-string permanently tied to the longer arm. Composite bows gave a much greater power-to-weight ratio than the 'self' bow, of which the longbow was the most famous version, with about twice the range. The compound curve or reflex shape reduced the actual height of the bow but permitted a very long draw, the composite construction also permitting a far greater pull than with a 'self' bow. The composite came in many versions, some being made only of laminated wood without other materials, while 'self' bows remained in use as hunting weapons among some Central Asian peoples. Meanwhile the composite bow evolved

over the centuries from a relatively long and cumbersome infantry weapon, through so-called Scythian, Parthian, Hunnish and Sassanian versions into the devastating Turkish cavalry bow of the High Middle Ages. Different types or weights were used for hunting or war, and while some peoples preferred long range, others concentrated on power of penetration or the number of arrows which could be loosed in a short period.

Bows could not be considered on their own for the weapon's character also depended on the type or weight of arrow, the bowstring, the use or otherwise of thumb-rings and various other factors. Arrows wholly or partly of reed would, for example, quickly absorb the vibration of being loosed and thus straightened out more quickly than wooden arrows. Yet some early Turks seem to have preferred wooden arrows for hunting. Such factors effected the type of quiver and bowcase carried. Two forms of the latter were used: while a long bowcase for one or more unstrung weapons tended to be more common in the early centuries and the broad bowcase for a strung weapon more

Various types of arrowhead: A-F—from Urals, 1st–5th C.; G-L—Tashtyk tribes, 1st–5th C.; M-N—Kokel tribes, southern Siberia, 2nd–5th C.; O—Kirghiz, 3rd–5th C.; P—Hun, 2nd–5th C.; Q—Kirghiz, 3rd–5th C.; R—Hun, 2nd–5th C.; S—Turk, 6th–10th C.; T—Hun, 2nd–5th C.; U—Turk, 6th–10th C.; V-W—Hun, 2nd–5th C.; X—Turk, 6th–10th C.; Y-Z—Huns in Europe, 5th C.; Aa-Bb—Turk, 6th–10th C.; Cc—Kirghiz, 6th–12th C.; Dd—Volga Bulgar, 8th–10th C.; Ee-Ff—East Turk, 7th–10th C.; Gg—Volga Bulgar, 8th–10th C.; Hh—Turk, 6th–10th C.

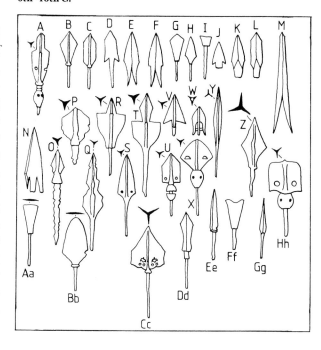

Gilt bronze plaques to decorate a saddle from Khakassia on the upper Yenisey River; Kirghiz, 9th century. The hunter uses a reflex bow, stirrups, and shoots rearwards with the so-called 'Parthian shot'. (Hermitage Mus., Leningrad)

Given the importance of archery among the nomads it is not surprising to find bows covered in gold being symbols of princely rank among the Huns. What is more surprising is that such impractical gilded weapons were not found among other peoples, not even among the Hsiung-Nu who are sometimes still regarded as the Huns' forebears. Gilded sword and dagger grips and guards were also characteristic of the Huns, while a gilded scabbard appears to have been reserved for princes among the Avars. The supposed scale pattern seen on the gilded decoration of Hun weapons and saddles may, in fact, reflect the feathers of the fabulous *simurgh* or *varanga* which decorate some late Sassanian Iranian weapons. Such fashions not only illustrate Sassanian influence but probably had a totemic function offering protection to the owner.

Swords

Although the curved sabre was known as the *gladius hunniscus* in Central Europe from the 8th century, there is no evidence that the Huns actually used single-edged sabres. Their swords were of the long double-edged Sassanian type suitable for cavalry warfare, also adopted by some Goths. Curved sabres may have been known in China as early as the 5th century while single-edged, but straight, 'proto-sabres' were soon the most common form of swords among steppe nomads. They were used in Europe by the Avars and Khazars, who despised any double-edged weapons offered as tribute. The curved sabre soon followed, but never entirely replaced the straight type.

Associated with developments in the sword was the hanging of a scabbard from a sword-belt. A scabbard-slide or loop fastened to the outside of a scabbard held the weapon vertically and was clearly designed to cope with heavier, longer cavalry swords which first appeared among the nomadic Iranian Kushans who had dominated eastern Iran. The scabbard-slide was then adopted by the Sassanian Iranians and many other Middle Eastern peoples, as well as by the later Romans, early Byzantines, various Germanic peoples and the Huns. The next major change was the hanging of a scabbard by two straps to a sword-belt. Designed to support a single-edged weapon at an

common later, both forms were used during most periods. A simple wooden 'self' bow gradually loses strength if permanently strung, though fully composite bows work better when kept under tension.

Of the two most common types of quiver, the short, open-ended, almost bag-like form seems to have been popular among professional cavalry around the fringes of the steppes, whereas the fully enclosed box-type appears to have been more popular among nomadic horse-archers or those only recently migrated into settled regions. The bag-like quiver would be more suitable for troops who seized their arrows 'by the bunch' and shot with that amazing rate characteristic of the best Middle Eastern horse-archers, while the box-type would be more suitable for men operating over long periods in areas with harsh climates who needed to protect their arrows. A form of fully enclosed quiver with a cap-like lid for infantry use appeared a little later and may have been of Chinese origin, though whether it had been used by Turkish infantry remains unclear. The Finno-Ugrian peoples of the northern forests certainly had a third type of quiver for use on foot: it was slung on the back, rather than from a belt, and was used while hunting on skiis. Even today it remains virtually impossible to link any form of arrowhead with specific tribes or peoples. The range of shapes is staggering, from the simplest, with or without barbs and spiked tangs or sockets, to those with three blades, with whistles at the rear, or with tiny grooves for poison.

adjustable angle, it was also much more convenient than a scabbard-slide when fighting on foot. The new system of straps first appeared in the eastern steppes and was associated with the Turks and possibly the Hephthalite or Eastern Huns.

Stone figure from Siberia; Turkish 8th century. Such carvings are found over graves in many areas inhabited by Turkish nomads. They are sometimes wrongly called *balbals* which were smaller uncarved stones standing around a warrior's grave. These carved figures probably portrayed the dead hero while the *balbals* represented his slain foes. (State Historical Mus., Moscow)

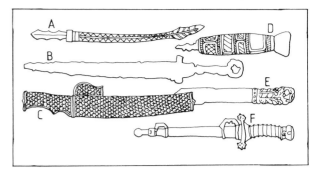

Daggers: A—Kokel peoples, southern Siberia 2nd–5th C. (ex-Khudyakov); B—possibly east-Hun Hephthalite, from Bahrein (location unknown); C—Sassanian Iran, 6th–7th C. (Met. Mus., New York); D—Pecheneg or Byzantine from Dinogetia-Garvan on the lower Danube, early 12th C. (ex-Diaconu); E—Ugrian western Siberia, 7th–13th C. (ex-Sedov); F—Alan from Martan-Chu, northern Caucasus, 9th C. (ex-Pletnyeva)

The 'Black' or Western Huns also used a second short-sword or large dagger, possibly descended from an ancient Iranian or Scythian short-sword, though it is likely that all such secondary weapons owed their ultimate origin to Central Asian fashion. Hung horizontally across the belly, it was adopted by Muslim warriors from their Transoxanian Turkish foes and became known as the *khanjar*. In Europe it probably lay behind the early medieval *seax* which remained a characteristic weapon of Germanic and Nordic peoples during the early Middle Ages.

Kirghiz, 9th century stone statue from Tuva. Note the Turkish sword-belt with pendant straps which became the mark of a military aristocracy as far west as Egypt and Hungary. (D. Vasilyev)

The Nomad and His Horse

The Turkish pony was a hardy beast, though small and ugly to the eyes of Westerners. Unlike the stall-fed horses of Europe it was able to survive harsh climates and live on grass alone. In general it was also better at climbing, jumping and swimming than medieval European horses. Steppe herds often interbred with wild horses and thus retained their vigour, nor was there only one type of steppe pony. Various peoples bred horses for travel, hunting or war, while others specialized in breeding for export.

The main characteristics looked for were a flat back for ease of riding and the long neck of a good jumper. The Chinese admired the 'celestial horses' of Central Asia, while the pony of 'dragon stock' was favoured by Turkish kings until they adopted the Arab horse after the Muslim conquests. 'Lord of the Horse' was a common title for Turkish rulers, and the bond between a warrior and his pony was comparable to that between the cowboy and his horse. The colour of an animal's hair also had great significance, the lightest colours being reserved for people of rank. Entire squadrons would be mounted on similar ponies, the Hsiung-Nu supposedly placing their bay or roan-mounted cavalry on the eastern frontier, while 'red' horses were deployed facing south, white to the west and black to the north. Dappled or piebald horses sometimes had almost magical significance. It may be no coincidence that in Christian myth the Four Horsemen of the Apocalypse rode horses which reversed the Far Eastern order of cosmic precedence, perhaps symbolizing the coming End of the World.

On a more prosaic level, many Eastern developments in horse harness were introduced to Europe by the steppe nomads. Certain elaborate types of bridle became common in Russia and may have reflected nomad influence. The wood-framed saddle, which was more comfortable to ride and much less wearing to a horse, had been known in China and Korea since the 5th century. An early version may have been used by the Huns, while the fully developed wood-framed saddle was copied from the Avars by Byzantines and western Europeans alike. The origins of the metal stirrup are still debated but it probably emerged in the frontier zone between China and the steppes. Primitive

Donor figure; wall painting from the Buddhist 'Cave of Sixteen Sword-bearers' at Kizil, early 7th century. This warrior reflects a part-Iranian, part-Turkish aristocracy which ruled the Central Asian oases in the early Middle Ages. (Staatliche Mus. Preuss. Kulturbesitz, West Berlin)

'toe-stirrups' of leather or rope loops had long been known in India, the western steppes and perhaps the Middle East, but the metal stirrup was almost certainly unknown to the Huns. Again it was the Avars who brought it west in the 6th and 7th centuries. Such stirrups were, of course, not essential to the horse-archer, though they did increase his repertoire of shots. Nor was it essential, as some historians still maintain, for cavalrymen who wielded lances or long swords. On the other hand it provided a firmer seat and increased a horse-soldier's effectiveness. Horseshoes were not favoured by steppe riders and did not become widespread before the Mongol conquest. Nomad cavalrymen also used whips rather than spurs to control their horses.

Decorations on harness and saddle were highly personal and remained remarkably traditional despite massive migrations, new religions and new artistic influences. Bronze pendants, or 'horse

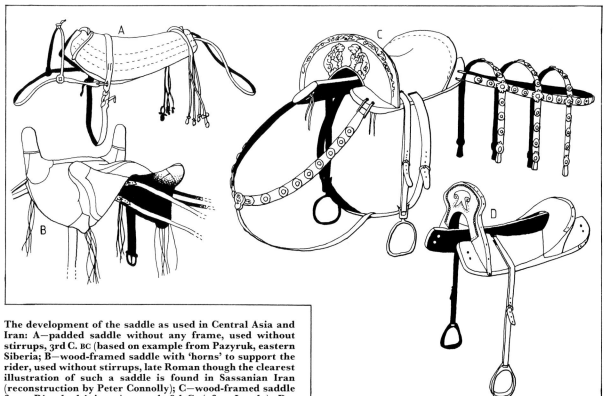

The development of the saddle as used in Central Asia and Iran: A—padded saddle without any frame, used without stirrups, 3rd C. BC (based on example from Pazyruk, eastern Siberia; B—wood-framed saddle with 'horns' to support the rider, used without stirrups, late Roman though the clearest illustration of such a saddle is found in Sassanian Iran (reconstruction by Peter Connolly); C—wood-framed saddle from Pérechtchépina, Avar, 7th–8th C. (after Laszlo); D—wood-framed saddle of nomad type with leather covering removed, from Zelenki near Kiev, 12th–13th C. (Hermitage Mus., Leningrad)

brasses', were particularly popular among Turkish warriors, as were tiny bells fastened to spear shafts. Decorative collars around a horse's neck spread from Iran to the Middle East, Central Asia and China. The *beçkem* or large tassel hanging from a horse's neck was originally the mark of a Turkish warrior elite but was eventually copied far to the west. The knotting of a horse's tail may have been associated with the animal's training but it also became characteristic of steppe and Turkish Middle Eastern warriors. One of the strangest means of grooming a horse was the trimming of its mane to produce a crenellated effect. The fashion probably appeared among the nomadic Kushans of eastern Iran, together with the scabbard-slide. It spread to the Iranian Sarmatian nomads of the western steppes and to T'ang China in the east. The fashion disappeared by the 8th century, after the coming of the Turks, although crenellated manes can still be seen on donkeys in parts of Afghanistan, and on horses in Turkey and the now largely Mongol Altai Mountains area. Many animals were branded with the tribal *tamga*, a

simple design which also appeared on weapons and belts. *Tamgas* were not, however, solely a Turco-Mongol idea, for the Indo-European Alan and Sarmatian nomads also branded their animals with such marks, many continuing to do so after they migrated into Europe and North Africa.

Transport

Though Central Asian peoples fought on horse-back and on foot, they also used two-humped Bactrian camels for transport. The Huns had no camels by the time they crossed the Carpathians into Central Europe, but camel-riding troops were recorded in the eastern oasis of Kuça in the 5th century and in a Western Turk army of the 7th. Such men would almost certainly have served as mounted infantry, riding camels for mobility but dismounting to fight. Indian war-elephants were used by Sassanian Iran, particularly in the east but occasionally in the west. Two hundred defended Ctesiphon against the Byzantines in the early 7th century, though few apparently remained to face the Muslim Arabs a generation later. A solitary war elephant was captured by the Muslims of

Kashgar from the Buddhist ruler of Khotan in the 10th century, the beast then being sent to the Emperor of China in AD 971. The use of war elephants in Khotan presumably reflected strong links between this Buddhist state in eastern Turkestan and India on the other side of the Karakoram Mountains.

Much more commonplace were the heavy waggons used by many nomadic and semi-nomadic Central Asian peoples to carry their homes, families and military supplies. Alans in the west, Toba in northern China, Huns, Turks, Bulgars and Kipchaqs all used this form of transport. Some waggons were very heavy and had iron tyres, a feature which was so exaggerated by early Byzantine chroniclers that those nomads who attacked Constantinople were credited with having iron carts! Far to the north the peoples of the forest and some of the steppe fringes used skis when hunting, though there is no reference to their being used in war.

The number of boats used by Turco-Mongol peoples may at first seem surprising. Most were, of course, small craft; but the rivers, lakes and inland seas of Central Asia are so immense that such craft could range from inflated skins and rafts to circular coracles, large skin-covered *umiak* or sleeker skin-covered *kayak* boats, dug-out and bark canoes and even fully planked ships. The boats and barges which the Toba used in China would, of course, have been Chinese, while the ships which a Sassanian-Avar-Slav alliance used against Byzantium would have been Mediterranean. These were sent against the walls of Constantinople and also seized the island of Rhodes in AD 652; while Slavs under Avar leadership had used their so-called 'canoes' to reach Crete in 623. The Turkish Khazars may have had sea-going ships on the Caspian, as well as the rivers of southern Russia, with which they attacked the Muslim city of Derbend. The Bulgars never challenged the Byzantines at sea even after reaching the Black Sea coast, yet in AD 827 they sent an army up the Danube, partly by boat, to force various Slav tribes into submission. Small wonder that Muslim Turks took to the sea so soon after conquering the coasts of Anatolia, eventually facing and almost defeating the combined fleets of the Christian western Mediterranean.

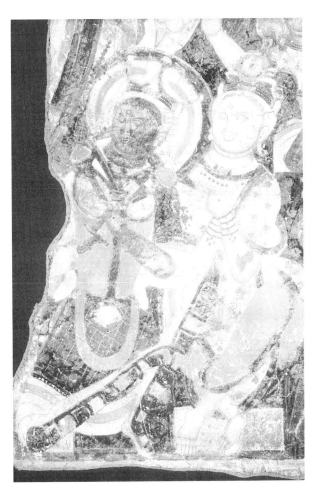

Wall painting from a small cave at Kizil, probably 7th century. This warrior listening to the Buddha seems to wear a quilted or soft armour. The defences which cover the front of his legs are more unusual and, like other Central Asian paintings in Indian style, this picture is highly stylized. (Staatliche Mus. Preuss. Kulturbesitz, West Berlin)

Fortifications

For supposedly barbarous nomads the peoples of Central Asia built fine fortifications. In the East these were inspired by Chinese methods. Many of the oasis trading towns were defended by stout walls; but whereas the Romans, Chinese and Iranians had developed a siege mentality behind 'long walls' or regularly spaced forts, watch-towers and beacons, the Turco-Mongol peoples preferred central citadels supported by scattered castles. Transoxania was, in particular, a land of many small but sophisticated fortifications with a few large walled cities. This system was again remarkably similar to that which developed in the medieval West, though a continued use of Chinese-

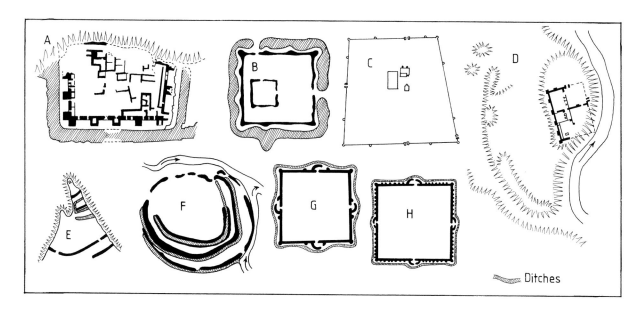

Fortifications: A—Igdui-Kala, Khwarazm, 4th–5th C. (after Tolstov); B—Uighur fortress, Tuva region, 8th–9th C. (after Pletnyeva); C—Citadel of Pliska, Bulgaria, 8th–9th C. (after Rashev); D—Alan-Khazar period fortress, Daghestan, 8th–10th C. (after Pletnyeva); E—Fort on spur of a hill, northern Caucasus 9th–13th C. (after Pletnyeva); F—Castle of Volga Bulgars, 10th–12th C. (after Pletnyeva); G-H—Small and large castles in Amur River region, 10th–13th C. (after Derevyanko)

style watch-towers and beacons found few parallels in a fragmented Europe.

Among western nomads the Avars were particularly renowned for their siege engines. Many were of Chinese type and were soon copied in the Middle East, Byzantium and Europe. The most important was the beam-sling mangonel, a man-

powered stone-throwing device which was easier to erect and operate than existing Graeco-Roman torsion engines. It would only be partially superseded by the Middle Eastern counterweight mangonel or *trebuchet* from the late 12th century. The Avars also used mobile wooden siege towers, movable sheds to protect miners and various other devices. The Bulgars inherited this tradition, and

Fortification reconstructions: A—section of wall of Balkh built by Turkish *yabgu* rulers, 7th–8th C. (after Esin); B—Gök Turk fortress of Sirdak-bek, Kashgar area (after Esin); C—Uighur fortress, Tuva region, 8th–9th C. (after Pletnyeva); D—Bulgar Khan's palace, Pliska, Bulgaria, 8th–9th C. (after Esin); E—earth and timber fortifications of Volga Bulgars, 10th–12th C. (after Esin); F—Karakhanid castle in Altai Mountains, 11th–12th C. (after Esin)

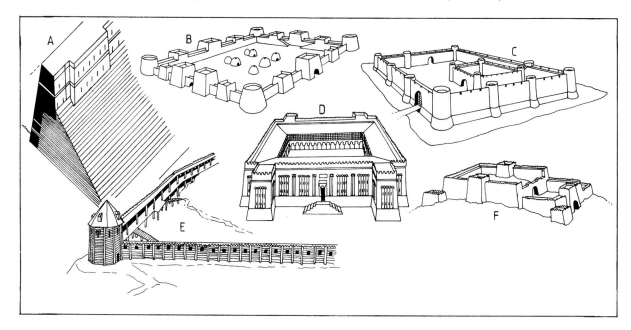

that of the Byzantines, to become masters of siege warfare by the 9th century.

The Byzantines helped friendly steppe states like that of the Khazars by designing fortifications at Sarkel on the lower Don River. Meanwhile the Abbasid Caliph of Baghdad sent his engineers to help the Volga Bulgars, enemies of the Khazars, erect their first large-scale fortifications. These, set amid the forests west of the Ural Mountains, were of timber and earth like those of medieval Russia. Oak walls were set above wood-framed, rubble-filled ramparts surrounded by deep ditches. Up to three rows of such ramparts and ditches protected major Volga Bulgar settlements. The later nomads of the western steppes built fewer defences. Yet they were well aware of the value of fortifications, the Pechenegs taking over many Byzantine castles along the Danube. Interestingly enough the Turkish Kipchaqs, the last nomads to invade eastern Europe before the coming of the Mongols, used an Arabic word for castle rather than a Turkish or Greek.

The Nomad Peoples

The Fountainhead
The regions north of China were the fountainhead of a remarkable number of migrations out of Central Asia and in the early years of the first millennium AD a nomadic people was again pressing against the Chinese frontier. These were the Hsiung-Nu, who are sometimes regarded as the mighty ancestors of the Huns. In fact their empire was very short-lived, having collapsed back in 36 BC. Thereafter the Hsiung-Nu remained as Chinese frontier 'allies', comparable to various Germanic peoples who served as Rome's frontier *feoderati*, before setting up ephemeral dynasties which were as rapidly overthrown by other petty rulers of Turco-Mongol origin.

The whole question of whether some Hsiung-Nu, perhaps mingling with nomads further west, eventually reappeared in eastern Europe as Huns remains unanswered. The Chinese described them as having almost Western features, while European chroniclers remark on the strong Asiatic appearance of the Huns. The Hsiung-Nu wore pigtails; the Huns did not but may have scarred their faces as warrior adornment. The Huns practised cranial deformation, making their skulls elongated, as did the Germans and Iranian Sarmatian nomads—but the Hsiung-Nu did not. The Huns, according to their foes, killed their own old folk, and lack of respect for the elderly characterized Indo-European peoples like the Germans and Alans but ran counter to east Asian tradition.

While the origins of the Huns remains obscure, other Central Asian peoples are better known. The partially Turkish Tashtyk of the upper Yenisi River, for example, remained in one place where they were both farmers and herdsmen. They used some Chinese forms of military equipment such as large rectangular infantry shields, and were rich in

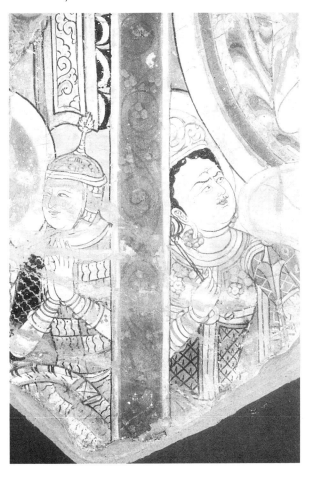

Warriors listening to the Buddha, cave paintings from Tumsuk, 7th century. Exotic and perhaps Indian forms of quilted armour on the right contrast with more realistic lamellar defences on the left. The armour on the left is shown with alternate rows of green and grey, reflecting the mixed iron and bronze construction found in surviving early medieval lamellar. (Staatliche Mus. Preuss. Kulturbesitz, West Berlin)

iron weaponry though archery remained their most important tactic. Tashtyk culture also had links with Iran and even Greece.

Better known are the Toba or Wei, a people of Turkish origin who founded the most effective 'barbarian' dynasties of early medieval China (AD 220–543). They succeeded because they retained their warlike nomad traditions while at the same time integrating themselves into China's sophisticated civilization. Much of the Toba nobility was separated from their tribes, living at court where they served as military officers. This also deprived the tribes of independent leadership. Some of the Toba's nomad foes were moved south into China where they also lost their tribal identity, becoming hereditary military units under

strict government control. Local armies seem to have been important in the ten Toba provinces, as were a highly developed postal system and a corps of 'censors' who kept strict watch on civil and military administration. The Chinese gentry proved more loyal than the tribal aristocracy and was soon entrusted with all aspects of government except the military, which remained in Toba hands. The Toba also inherited advanced Chinese arms production centres and transport systems where the Chinese themselves had a military rôle to play. Meanwhile Toba armies gradually used greater numbers of infantry, most of whom were probably Chinese rather than Turco-Mongol.

High casualties among the Toba ruling elite and neglect of the horse-herds after the Toba capital moved south to Loyang also undermined the Toba's own military domination. Unable to conquer southern China, the Toba turned west, seizing control of much of the rich Silk Road linking China to the Middle East and gobbling up other minor dynasties until they had unified northern China for the first time in centuries. This also enabled them to recruit additional nomad troops from their defeated foes. Despite an increasing reliance on Chinese infantry, Toba cavalry were still able to defeat the formidable Juan-Juan in the mid-5th century. Nevertheless the Juan-Juan (meaning in Chinese 'nasty wriggling insects') continued to rule over a loose confederation of tribes stretching from Mongolia to Lake Balkash. Around AD 550 they were overthrown by their previous subjects, the Turks, thus setting off another wave of tribal movements when 30,000 Juan-Juan 'tents' or families migrated west to reach Europe as the Avars.

The Huns and their Successors

Whether or not they were descended from the Hsiung-Nu, the Huns had a devastating impact on the settled civilizations of the Middle East and Mediterranean. They were basically divided into the Hephthalite or 'White' Huns who invaded Iran and the 'Black' Huns who attacked Europe.

The Hephthalites may have been more Mongol than Turkish in origin and even their various invasions of Transoxania, Afghanistan and Iran remain obscure. They were clearly a powerful force in eastern Iran by the 5th and early 6th

Brassière-like armours in early Central Asian and Chinese art also appear in Mongol-Islamic art of the 14th century. They probably reflect a shaped or more flexible chest area to ease breathing. Here it is worn by a soldier of King Mara on a wall painting from the Buddhist 'Stairs Cave' at Kizil, early 7th century. (Staatliche Mus. Preuss. Kulturbesitz, West Berlin)

The gold ewer from the Nagyszentmiklos Treasure remains a mystery. Is it Germanic Goth from the time of the Great Migrations, early Hungarian, 10th century Khazar, or made north of Iran in the 8th–9th century? The armoured horseman has a segmented helmet with a separate coif or aventail, a full mail hauberk with splinted arm and leg defences similar to those seen in early Scandinavia or Anglo-Saxon England. But limb armour was also common in early medieval Transoxania, Armenia and the Muslim world. Neither this mailed rider nor the horse-archer uses stirrups but the latter may wear quilted soft armour and has headgear like the stylized 'infidel' turbans shown in Byzantine Russian art. This, and the decoration, suggest the ewer was made under early Islamic, Byzantine and Turkish influences in the Caucasus region between the 7th and 10th centuries. (Kunsthistorisches Mus., VII.B33, Vienna)

centuries, fielding armies which differed from those of the Huns in Europe. 'Red' Huns as well as the 'White' Hephthalites are also recorded in this war-torn period, but neither appear to have remained nomads, and they supposedly had fair complexions compared to the steppe nomads of the north. Their language was a form of Turkish and they fought with long-hilted, long-bladed straight swords and composite bows but no stirrups. Some of those who invaded India set up minor principalities in the Punjab which survived to the early 7th century, while some of their Kushan predecessors had also remained east of the Indus for some centuries. Though crushed between a revived Sassanian Empire and the newly arrived Turks, other Hephthalite princes remained in Afghanistan which flourished as a centre of Buddhist culture. Yet these descendants of the fearsome Huns did not lose their warrior skills, for this area put up a remarkably successful resistance to the Muslims well into the early 8th century.

The 'Black' Huns who conquered the Russian steppes around AD 370 seemed to have sprung from nowhere, yet they were not as unknown as Roman chroniclers claimed, Huns having lived north-east of the Black Sea before the 2nd century. Neverthe-less a terrified Roman world invented fantastic legends to account for their sudden eruption. Some borrowed from ancient Greek myth to claim that the Huns followed a deer across the Cimmerian Straits, while others dug into Christian demonology to explain that the Huns were descended from fallen angels and witches. Whoever they were, these 'Black' Huns overthrew the existing order. Germanic Goths who dominated areas west of the Dnepr River, Iranian-speaking Sarmatian and Alan nomads to the east and the Greek-speaking Bosphoran kingdom around the Crimea all collapsed within a few years. Some fled deeper into Europe while others remained under Hun rule. Early in the 5th century the Huns crossed the Carpathians into the Hungarian Plain, and in AD 434 their vast realm was unified under a new leader—Attila.

While in southern Russia the Hun army seems to have been a typical steppe nomadic force. They

A crudely inscribed clay tile from Madara in Bulgaria. Probably 7th century early Bulgar, it shows a warrior with a segmented helmet and a lamellar cuirass with the brassière-like chest protection seen in Central Asian art.

Attila's campaigns were more Germanic than nomad in character, particularly those undertaken in summer, which would have been almost unthinkable for a steppe army. Roman sources no longer emphasized massed Hun cavalry, and by the late 4th century Hun horses are rarely mentioned at all. Of course Hun cavalry did exist, and its armoured elite fought with long spears as well as bows. Huns are also described as dismounting to fight, as serving as infantry archers, and as carrying shields large enough to lean upon; such shields inevitably bring to mind those of Tashtyk and Toba infantry. When worsted the Hun army now tended to retreat into its camp rather than dispersing at high speed as was normal for nomad cavalry. Other sources make it quite clear that the Huns increasingly relied on infantry in Europe and that they fielded a siege train which might have been operated by Roman renegades. In fact a major part of Attila's army was clearly of German or Alan origin and the name Hun, in Roman chronicles, must refer to political rather than ethnic origin.

The Huns in Europe now lived by predation, in other words raiding, rather than nomadism. Society was still tribal, with each tribe apparently sub-divided into clans or families under its own aristocratic leadership. Prisoners were generally ransomed as the Huns, unlike the Romans, had little need for slaves, while those who remained in their hands could even rise to prominence. There is unlikely to have been a large social gap between a free warrior and his chief but there were degrees of status at Attila's court. Roman commentators referred to Attila's *logades*, 'friends' or 'companions', many of whom had German names. Their rôle is unclear but they were probably prominent men rather than a military aristocracy. Other Germanic leaders in Attila's army may have led mercenary bands. Such a state was more Germanic than Turco-Mongol and had little in common with the empires of the steppes. The Huns also appear to have been on the verge of converting to Christianity when their empire suddenly collapsed. On Attila's death in AD 453 the realm was divided among his sons, who promptly started a civil war. Their German subjects rose in rebellion and within a year the surviving Huns retreated back to the steppes of southern Russia.

used lassos, as did most nomads whether of Turkish or Iranian origin, and they adopted many fashions from those Alans whom they now ruled. But almost everything seems to have changed once the Huns moved out of the steppes into the Hungarian Plain. They lost their nomad logistical base, and their success in raiding Roman territory probably owed more to a lack of effective opposition than to a continued use of Central Asian military styles. Only a minority of Huns would have worn armour but those who later served as mercenaries in Rome and Byzantium were expected to arm themselves. Like their predecessors they probably captured or purchased Romano-Byzantine or Goth equipment. Nevertheless, iron cuirasses and a few gilded helmets are mentioned during Attila's time. Even

The chaos that they left is part of another story, but the Huns did not degenerate into a band of 'squalid brigands' as some historians claim. Under Attila's descendants many returned to nomadism but continued to raid the East Roman Empire. Others settled down inside Roman territory, garrisoning various areas as *feoderati*, while yet others simply served as mercenaries in the last armies of the West Roman Empire.

While the Germans seized their independence in the west, the Alans had already recovered theirs in the east. By now these Iranian-speaking nomads were virtually identical to the Huns in tactics and military equipment. They had always used repeated attacks and feigned retreat to trap a foe, but they now seem to have abandoned their traditional javelins in favour of bows while still using heavy spears and long swords. The Alans would remain a potent force despite gradually being forced out of the steppes and into the Caucasus Mountains by Bulgar, Turkish and Khazar invaders. There they remained, converting to Christianity in the 6th century, colonizing the valleys and developing an almost feudal society around numerous rocky castles. These later Alans produced highly decorated weapons, embroidered leather horse-harness and gilded bridle-bits. Warlike as ever, they served as mercenaries in Byzantium as late as the 14th century and their Ossetian descendants still inhabit parts of Georgia.

The Bosphoran Kingdom never regained its independence. Instead the Byzantines took control of the south Crimean coast while survivors of the Germanic Goth population inhabited the mountains. Another people to re-emerge from the wreck of the Hun empire were the Sabirs, who were themselves of Hun or Turkish origin. They took much of the steppe between the Black and Caspian Seas where, like the Alans, they played a rôle in the unending struggle between Byzantium and the Sassanian Empire. Some were later settled by the Byzantines in eastern Anatolia as one of the first Turkish groups to colonize this region. In the late 6th century those Sabirs north of the Caucasus were crushed by the Avars, their survivors again being pushed into the mountains, where they eventually converted to Islam and merged with the present-day peoples of Daghestan.

The Turks

Of all the peoples who stemmed from Central Asia none made a greater impact than the Turks. First known in Chinese as T'u-chüeh, their name may have meant 'helmet', and they seem to have been a minor tribe specializing in iron-working amid the Altai Mountains. Their origins were clearly very mixed; but after defeating the Juan-Juan they unified almost all the nomad peoples of eastern Central Asia under their Gök, 'Blue' or 'Celestial', Khaganate. Around AD 583 this vast empire divided into the generally hostile Eastern and Western Khaganates.

Echoes of almost forgotten wars between Gök Turks and Sassanians are heard in the great Iranian national poem, the *Shahnamah*, and the tactics of these warlike people were, of course, based on horse-archery. The Turks were, however, particularly well organized and disciplined. According to the Chinese they drew up in ordered ranks before attacking and would then adopt an arrowhead formation as they charged. The Turks used whistling arrows, perhaps for communicating orders, and would fight in close combat with curved and straight swords, daggers and spears. Their use of two-humped Bactrian camels suggests an important rôle for mobile mounted infantry while thousands of mercenary soldiers, sometimes paid with lengths of Chinese silk, were recruited from other regions.

Turkish military ritual was also highly developed. Before a campaign new drums and drum-

Carved on a rock-face near Madara is an early Bulgarian ruler, now believed to be Khan Tervel (AD 701–718). Such rock-reliefs were typical of Sassanian Iran and they show how strong Iranian influence was on nomadic cultures as far west as the Balkans.

skins would be prepared, no expedition being possible until these instruments struck the correct note. Meanwhile warriors would go hunting for a skin to be made into a *suluk* or small 'kit-bag' attached to the right side of a sword-belt. A slaughtered sheep would then be hung, one half on each side of the saddle, as food for the next weeks. Horses' tails would be knotted, animals and riders both being decorated with silk badges, tufts of hair or feathers. The leader's 'silken dome' tent would be prepared, drums beaten and banners raised, whereupon the warriors made a great shout and shot arrows into the air. Thus a pre-Islamic Turkish army was readied for war. Mounted military bands with drums, cymbals, horns and bells played a vital rôle in communicating orders, maintaining morale and as a symbol of authority. In fact the Khagan had his own orchestra of 80 or so musicians.

Unlike the Huns, the Turks took the hair rather than the heads of their slain foes. They were notably well equipped: their armour was of metal or hardened leather lamellae (*say yarik*), with a little mail (*küpe yarik*) and a variety of helmets. Elite heavy cavalry used horse-armour (*kedimli*),

while the dress of a military leader could be particularly splendid. One West Turk prince, captured by the Arabs in AD 739, wore a heavy lamellar cuirass, brocade-covered leggings and a long silk tunic lined with brocade. Other Turkish garments included shorter tunics, weather-proofed quilted coats, breeches, boots, sandals for walking, various hats and either long-sleeved or sleeveless cloaks. Riding boots could be of felt, fur or fabric. Some were pulled right up the leg like hose; others appear to have been attached to the saddle rather than the rider, who would presumably step into them as he mounted. Among the aristocracy both men and women wore jewellery, while guard units would be dressed in a single colour such as red or orange silk, similar to the ruler's flags and the saddle-covers of his courtiers.

Only those warriors skilled at shooting backwards as well as forwards were permitted to put white falcon wings or feathers in their helmets while doubled gilded and fabric belts, decorated with pendants, were another mark of rank among *tarkans* or 'heroes'. Elaborate *tug* 'tailed' banners or horse-tails were carried separately or attached to the ruler's great drums. Totemic tribal ensigns were known as *tös* while smaller individual *badrak* pennons were attached to spear-shafts. Horse-tail banners indicated a leader's status, as they would continue to do until the 18th century in the Ottoman Empire—five, seven or nine horse-tails being the usual number. Gilded wolf, dragon and other mask-banners were, however, reserved for the Khagan himself among the Gök Turks as well as later Turks and Uighurs.

The influence of Turkish ceremonial was as wide as that of their arms, armour and tactics. In the Khagan's court certain actions and gestures indicated homage or status, and this seems to have been particularly the case where a military elite was concerned. Before the Turks converted to Islam their society was very hierarchic, with the Khagan standing as a semi-divine link between heaven and earth. Such a rôle was symbolized by

Stone funerary statues: A—Turkish from Altai Mountains, 6th–10th C. (ex-Pletnyeva); B—East Turkish from Altan-Sandal, Mongolia, 7th–8th C. (ex-Nowgorodowa); C—unknown nomad origin from Zlatna niva, Bulgaria, 7th–12th C. (Local Museum, Shumen); D—Pecheneg or Kipchaq from Dnepr region, 12th C. (ex-Pletnyeva); E—Pecheneg from Dnepr region, 11th–12th C. (ex-Pletnyeva); F-G—Pecheneg or Kipchaq from Dnepr region, 12th C. (ex-Pletnyeva)

On this Uighur wall painting from 8th–9th century Kumtura a Chinese dignitary is seized by two soldiers wearing Turkish lamellar armour, one riding an armoured horse and wielding a straight sword. They probably portray Uighur heavy cavalry with great accuracy. (Staatliche Mus. Preuss. Kultur-besitz, West Berlin)

his silk parasols and his great tent which, among the Gök Turks, was of red silk decorated with embroidered flowers and supported by gilded poles. It could hold hundreds of people, numerous beds and even waggons, while totemic standards stood around its door. A ruler's throne was also gilded, that of the Gök Turk Khagan being supported by four carved peacocks; those of the rulers of Farghana and Bukhara were supported by a ram and a camel. Even hair styles were significant, the long plaits of a warrior being tied with various coloured ribbons. Junior warriors would sometimes shave the fronts of their heads as a sign of submission to their elders, and a top-knot was a mark of mastery among some tribes. Hats with upturned brims signified rank, and different ways of kneeling before the ruler were reserved for people of varying ranks: going down on one knee indicated high status and readiness to serve, going down on both knees indicated humility and menial status. Even the positioning of hands across the breast or beside the body was symbolic.

The splitting of the Gök Turk Khaganate into Eastern and Western states inevitably undermined Turkish power, and the Eastern Turks soon clashed with a China which had revived under the native T'ang dynasty. Eastern Turk armies relied increasingly on heavily armoured cavalry, though the bow remained their main weapon, and they could be static enough for a Chinese army to overwhelm their camp in a night attack. While the Eastern Turks settled down to agriculture and urban life, the Western Turks retained their nomad ways for longer. Their military tactics also remained traditional. According to a Chinese ambassador the ruler's guards were dressed in fur and woollen cloth, their spears, banners and bows being in excellent condition, their ranks of horses and camels stretching far out of sight, while their Khagan sat in a tent decorated with golden flowers. Reference to camels again indicated the use of mounted infantry. Even a local khan might wear a green silk cloak, his unplaited hair being bound with a long piece of silk in the style of 'settled' rather than nomadic peoples. It was these

25

who in turn overthrew the Eastern Turkish realm. Others would later play a major rôle in southern Russia (see below), and their vital rôle in Muslim armies is well known (see MAA 125 *The Armies of Islam 7th–11th Centuries*). Most clung to their traditions of horse-archery and were regarded by both Byzantines and Muslims as vulnerable if they ran out of arrows.

Those Turks who had earlier settled in Transoxania were, in some respects, distinct from the Western Turkish Khaganate of the steppes. Some were assimilated into existing Iranian or Hephthalite aristocracies while others retained a Turkish identity as a local military elite. Generally known as 'Türgish', most were independent of the Western Turkish Khagan by the time the Muslim Arabs reached Transoxania. The region was divided into five rich but warlike principalities under an elite which bore various obscure titles. The *yabgu* of what is now northern Afghanistan was taken to Damascus as a captive in AD 724. The *afshin* of Ushrusana in the Syr Darya valley was among the first to serve the conquering Muslims in a military capacity, taking his Buddhist and Manichean idols and paintings to Samarra in

Another 9th century wall painting from Temple No. 9, Bezeklik, shows Uighur princes in court costume. Despite Chinese influence the fashions remain distinctly Turkish. (Staatliche Mus. Preuss. Kulturbesitz, West Berlin)

Metalwork: silver dish from Kulagysh, Sassanian Iran or Transoxania, 7th–8th C., note similarity with foot combat on wall-painting from Piandjikent (Hermitage Mus., Leningrad); bronze jar from Iran or Transoxania, late Sassanian or early Islamic, 6th–8th C. (Met. Mus. of Art, New York); C—silver dish, Transoxanian, 8th–9th C. (Hermitage Mus., Leningrad); D—silver bowl from Ural Mountains, eastern Magyar, 9th C. (Hermitage Mus., Leningrad)

Western Turks who bore the brunt of the first Arab Islamic thrusts into Central Asia as well as attacks by the T'ang Chinese. Only in AD 740 did the Western Turkish Khaganate finally collapse, and thereafter the Western Turks were better known as the Oghuz.

Some Oghuz tribes had infiltrated eastern Iran during the confusion of the Islamic conquest and these soon became Muslim. So, more gradually, did Oghuz tribes along Islam's newly stabilized Central Asian frontier. Others migrated further west to settle in Byzantine Anatolia in the 8th century. Those in the east became the Uighurs,

Attackers and defenders from siege scene on a silver repoussé dish from Malo-Amkovkaya, Turkish Transoxania or Semirecye, 9th–10th C. (Hermitage Mus., Leningrad)

advanced than the castles of Iran itself. Mud-brick was the favoured building material in the lowlands, stone being used in the mountains while Chinese architectural influence could also be seen in some aspects of fortification. Transoxania exported military goods, the war horses of Farghana being particularly highly regarded while Transoxanian armours were fine and abundant enough for the 'forges of Sughd' to enter Islamic mythology.

Türgish tactics were, however, Turkish rather than Iranian. Their arms and armour, despite the impression created by wall paintings in palaces like Piandjikent, were lighter than those of Iranians or Arabs. In battle against an early 8th century Muslim governor an army was drawn up with the ruler's guard holding a hill in the centre, allied Turkish tribes holding the right and dissident Muslims the left. An arrow could be shot across a river as a challenge to battle and a herd of sheep might be stampeded through an enemy's camp during a night attack in an attempt to panic the foe. Repeated charges by mounted archers remained the basic tactic; horses being trained not to 'swerve aside' but remain running in a straight line until turned by a touch of the bridle—not by pressure of the rider's legs as some suggest. Troops from cities like Bukhara seem to have served as infantry archers, and the Türgish clearly used all the normal methods of siege warfare. By thus drawing on the traditions of Iran, China and Central Asia the military elite of Transoxania became one of the most sophisticated in Asia.

The Second Wave

Among the Hun tribes who remained in the south Russian steppes after the collapse of Attila's empire were the Onogurs (people of 'Ten Arrows') who, as the Bulgars (meaning 'mixed people'), gradually created the state of Old Bulgaria around the Sea of Azov. The Onogurs had also been in close association with the Magyars, a forest-dwelling people of Finno-Ugrian origin who eventually set off on their own to create the new nation of Hungary (see MAA 150 *The Age of Charlemagne*). To further confuse the issue the term 'Hungarian' may actually stem from Onogur!

Iraq. Other Türgish elite were called *sad*, which may have been a military title.

Transoxanian military styles have been described as similar to those of Sassanian Iran; this is misleading, for the Sassanians were themselves under strong Central Asia influence through Transoxania. Supposedly 'gladiatorial' combats marking the New Year in Farghana at the head of the Syr Darya valley, as well as horse-archery contests during religious celebrations, have few parallels in Iran, while the prominent rôle of military music among the Türgish is clearly Turkish. On the other hand the advanced fortifications which dotted this area seem to have been in the Iranian tradition, though in many respects more

Old Bulgaria was under Hun-Bulgar domination and was ruled by a dynasty possibly claiming descent from Attila, but Alans and Slavs also played a prominent role in its military affairs. Little is known of Old Bulgar armies except that they were similar to those of the succeeding Khazars. Other Bulgar tribes included the Utigurs and Kutrigurs who, together with Slavs, raided deep inside the Byzantine Balkans in the late 5th century. The collapse of Old Bulgaria and the scattering of the Bulgar people paradoxically simplified this chaos of names and misnomers. Some remained in southern Russia to be absorbed by the victorious Khazars, while others migrated north into the forests where they became known as

Uighur temple banner, 9th century from Toyok. Here a Buddhist *lokapala* wears a lamellar cuirass, loose trousers and holds a composite bow. (Staatliche Mus. Preuss. Kulturbesitz, West Berlin)

Volga Bulgars (see below). Those who fled under Onogur leadership into the Balkans may have included the military elite of Old Bulgaria. They eventually established the nation we still know as Bulgaria. By the late 6th century these Balkan Bulgars, like the Balkan Slavs, had fallen under the domination of yet another wave of nomads—the Avars—but this merely encouraged their aggression against the Byzantines. They may have captured Corinth for a short time in the 640s, possibly leaving some of their men in shallow graves beneath the Citadel, along with military artifacts showing both Byzantine and nomadic influence. The Bulgars who settled along the Danube were soon absorbed by their Slav subjects, leaving little more than their name behind.

The Avars who, for a time, dominated the Balkan Bulgars were descended from the Juan-Juan of the eastern steppes though they may also have included some Hephthalite Huns from eastern Iran. Like the Huns before them the Avars pushed on into Europe, making the Hungarian Plain their base. They were of Mongoloid appearance, wore long pigtails like the Hsiung-Nu, and brought a fully developed state organization from the East. By no stretch of the imagination could these Avars be called barbarian and in military matters they were generally in advance of their foes. Though mobile they were no longer nomadic by the time they reached Central Europe. The Avar capital was a tent city, rich in gold and weapons, and the state was surrounded by a series of *hring* citadels based upon existing fortresses of Roman Pannonia.

Avar strategy rested on raiding rather than further conquest and archaeological evidence suggests that they had more horses than did Attila's Huns. Armoured cavalry played a dominant rôle but the Avar army included many Slav infantry. The sieges of Byzantine Thessaloniki and Constantinople show that the Avars possessed efficient and abundant siege engines, plus the men to operate them. Like the Turks, the Avar elite cavalry fought with bow and spear, being protected by iron lamellar or heavy felt armour. Avar horse-armour was also of lamellar or felt and apparently only covered the animal's head, neck and forequarters. A singular Avar item of cavalry armour was a form of neck-protecting gorget, perhaps similar to those seen in Chinese and Central Asian tomb figures. The Avar composite bow was clearly descended from a Chinese type and was more curved and possibly shorter than that used by the Huns. The Avars also used single-edged though generally straight swords. An obscure cord fastened to the centre of Avar spears was probably a wrist-strap.

For most Europeans the Avars are less well known than the Huns, yet their military and cultural influence was far greater. Avar heavy cavalry served as an ideal among the Byzantines for many years. It was from them that the Byzantines adopted the stirrup, probably the wood-framed military saddle and a more powerful bow. They also copied the Avars' loose fitting cavalry tunic, the neck-protecting *stroggulion* 'gorget', the cavalry lance with its additional strap, as well as new forms of horse-armour, tents and beam-sling mangonel siege machines. The military sub-divisions of the Avar state may even have influenced the development of the Byzantine system of *themes* or military provinces. Western Europe similarly learned new cavalry techniques from the Avars, though the Muslims of Spain and the Magyars who conquered Hungary some generations later also played a part.

The Khazar Turks who seized the Russian steppes in the 670s are best remembered because their ruling elite converted to Judaism a century later. Like many steppe peoples the Khazars were of mixed origins but their state endured longer than that of most. Even before the Muslim Arabs appeared on their southern frontier the Khazars had allied themselves with Byzantium against Sassanian Iran and this traditional friendship continued after the Sassanians collapsed. The Arabs proved to be much more formidable neighbours and this clash forced the Khazars to move their Caucasus capital north to the mouth of the Volga. Originally shamanist, the Khazars almost converted to Islam following a shattering defeat by an Arab army which chased the Khazar Khagan right across the steppes into the forests of the north. Instead, however, the Khagan went back on his agreement and revived the Khazar alliance with Byzantium. A short time later the ruling elite converted to Judaism, though the number of converts remains a matter of heated debate. Others adopted Christianity or turned to Islam

A damaged drawing from Yarkhoto probably illustrates an Uighur warrior carrying a white banner. His bowcase is designed for a strung weapon, his sword has a slight curve and he appears to have the armour of his lower right arm loosened. (Staatliche Mus. Preuss. Kulturbesitz, MIK III 17, West Berlin)

which most Khazars accepted after the collapse of their state in the early 11th century.

The long history of the Khazars inevitably made them different from more ephemeral nomad states. Trading cities developed along the great rivers that crossed Khazar territory, though most consisted of tents and flimsy wooden structures with few brick buildings. Apart from the Turkic Khazar people themselves another twenty-five subject tribes sent hostages to the Khagan's court, among them Finno-Ugrians and Slavs from the northern forests and Iranian-speaking peoples from the Caucasus. The true Khazars were semi-nomadic, wintering in tent cities, tending their herds in distant pastures during the summer and engaging in agriculture or fishing. The Khazar army also changed over the centuries, the long-haired massed tribal cavalry of the early days being supplemented by heavily armoured horsemen with swords and lances. By the early 10th century these men, wearing helmets, mail hauberks and lamellar cuirasses, formed a standing army of full-time professionals. The later Khazar army also included the Khagan's trusted bodyguard of about 7,000 Muslim mercenaries from Khwarazm in the north of Transoxania. Khazars themselves, of course, had already served outside their own frontiers. Khazar prisoners were recruited by the Sassanians of Iran in the early days while Khazar mercenaries fought for Byzantium on many occasions.

The Silk Road

The trading routes or Silk Roads across Central Asia brought great wealth to this area but also attracted the attention of neighbouring empires. Some of the oasis staging posts, like Kuça, were ruled by local princes who paid tribute to China in an effort to maintain their independence. Their varied populations included peoples of Iranian nomad origin, Turks and Mongols. Merchants from Tibet, India, China and Transoxania flocked to their bazaars while troops seem to have been recruited from equally varied sources. Chinese aggression revived under the T'ang dynasty which seized the entire area as far west as Lake Balkash in the 7th and 8th centuries, but the Muslim conquest of Transoxania changed the balance of power. T'ang authority collapsed; nomad empires rose and fell but throughout it all the oases of Central Asia enjoyed prosperity and flourishing trade. For a while Tibet also expanded northwards, almost isolating the eastern oases around Khotan which were apparently independent until the 10th century. The Khotanese were themselves descended from nomadic Iranian Sakas but, because of their Buddhist religion, were in closer contact with India. In fact Khotan became a major centre of Buddhist culture and resisted Muslim expansion for centuries.

The armies of such oasis principalities were small but seem to have been richly equipped. It needed 70,000 Chinese infantry and 5,000 cavalry to conquer Kuça in the late 4th century. In the face of such a massive invasion the ruler of Kuça and his vassals retreated to various castles, leaving a garrison to defend the oasis city. This they did by inflating their numbers with fully armoured wooden dummies manning various sections of the wall. The ruler of Kuça then attempted to relieve the oasis with a vast relief army, supposedly of 200,000 men, which must have been recruited from neighbouring nomads. Following other Chinese campaigns in the 7th century, captured Turks and Sughdians from Transoxania were settled in the Ordos region of northern China. Less than a century later descendants of these prisoners were reported in the army of the Chinese rebel Lu-shan who shook the T'ang dynasty to its foundations. In fact Sughdians had a big impact on China, introducing western religions like Christianity and influencing the design of a huge new Chinese capital at Ch'ang-an.

Faced with the Lu-shan rebellion, the Chinese T'ang dynasty found allies among the Uighurs. This Turkish people, descended from the Oghuz Western Turks, led a confederation of nine tribes which conquered most of eastern Turkestan, drove out the Tibetans and built a state which became

A fragmentary 8th century painted silk from Koço carries a Manichaean text and two warriors whose helmets have short nasals. (Staatliche Mus. Preuss. Kulturbesitz, MIK III 6279, West Berlin)

famous for its culture as well as its military might. The Uighur capital was renowned for its massive castle with two iron-clad gates. On top of this fortress stood the Khagan's gold silk tent which, imported from China, could hold a hundred people and was visible for miles. An Uighur Khagan of AD 758 was described as wearing a yellow-ochre robe, a 'barbarian' hat and being surrounded by his guards. Like all Turkish tribes, the Uighurs had originally been nomad horse-archers, at which time their encampment consisted of a circle formed by the army's tents with those of the ruler in the centre. Four gaps or lanes led through these tents to an area of pasture where the horses grazed while beyond was another ring formed by the tents of seventeen subordinate chiefs, each with as many followers as the ruler himself. By the mid-8th century the Uighurs had largely settled in cities, villages or iron-mining communities and an Uighur army of AD 765 included many infantry as well as cavalry. Yet it was the heavily armoured horse-archers who impressed the Chinese. In AD 835 the Uighurs even sent seven women horse-archers to be attendants upon a Chinese princess—though that lady's reaction remains unrecorded!

The speed of manoeuvre, ferocity and looting of Uighur troops remained undiminished, though they could be defeated. In AD 784, in alliance with the T'ang, they attacked a rebel army which had taken position on high ground. First the Uighurs struck from the front and then from the rear. This time, however, the Chinese rebels not only turned to face the second attack but managed to catch their enemies in an ambush by additional troops stationed further back. Like other Turks, Uighur warriors wore their hair long and compared their tresses to a lion's mane. The elite was dressed in Chinese silk, this being one way in which the T'ang paid for Uighur military assistance. Many of their banners were white and they used 'rain stones', those magical pebbles which were believed to influence the weather in an army's favour. The Uighurs are also widely credited with 'civilizing' the Turkish nomads. As a famous Manichean inscription in the Uighur capital of Karabalgasun stated: 'a country of barbarous customs, full of the fumes of blood, was changed into a land where the people live on vegetables; from a land of killing to a

Warriors with mail or lamellar aventails over their faces were more characteristic of the western steppes, Transoxania and Muslim Iran than the Uighur east. Fragment from Koço, 8th or 9th century. (Staatliche Mus. Preuss. Kulturbesitz, MIK III 6330, West Berlin)

land where good deeds are fostered.' The Uighur people survived the overthrow of the Khagan by the Kirghiz and recreated two smaller principalities which survived for several more centuries.

West of the Tien Shan Mountains another Turkish people, the Qarluks, inherited the struggle against the advancing Arab Muslims. Their *yab-*

Bronze harness decorations: A—Hsiung-Nu from Ordos region, 4th–5th C. (ex-Egami); B—Turkish 6th–10th C. (ex-Khudyakov); C—Kirghiz, 6th–8th C. (ex-Khudyakov); D-E—Kimak, 9th–10th C. (ex-Khudyakov); F—Kirghiz, 6th–8th C. (ex-Khudyakov)

ghus or kings welcomed both Sughdian refugees and dissident Muslims, supported rebellions within Muslim territory but, at the same time, permitted the spread of Islam among their own people. Nestorian Christianity also made converts, particularly in Semirecye south of Lake Balkash. As a result of this penetration by Middle Eastern cultures, the Qarluks were soon more advanced than other nomad peoples north of the Tien-Shan and Altai mountains, though they remained a tribal confederation rather than a unified state. Information about Qarluk military organization is, however, very sketchy. The numbers of warriors available from the trading towns within Qarluk territory ranged from the 80,000 of Suyab (now Kara-bulaq), which was governed by a man known as the *Yalan-Shah* or 'King of Heroes', to the 3,000 raised from Yar, headquarters of the Jil tribe. Arab geographers list six such centres raising no less than 47,000 troops who also seem to have been renowned for wearing red clothes.

To the north of the Qarluks lived the Kimaks, an even more obscure and certainly more primitive nomadic people. They inhabited the northern fringes of the steppes east of the Ural Mountains. These Kimaks had close links with the Oghuz to their south, built underground villages against the winter cold but had no towns and never became Muslim. They provided a vital link in the fur-trade from the far north and made numerous funerary statues, though of wood rather than stone. It was also from these Kimaks that the warlike Kipchaqs would later spring to conquer deep into Russia and the Balkans.

Far more important in military, political and culture terms were the Karakhanids, yet even they remain among the least known of Muslim dynasties. Emerging from the Qarluk tribal association in the 9th century they were converted to Islam in the 10th. By the end of that century these powerful Turkish khans controlled a loose confederation on both sides of the Tien Shan Mountains. From the mid-11th century, however, there were effectively two Karakhanid states, one on each side of the mountains. Under their rule the Turkification of Transoxania gathered pace while Islam spread into eastern Turkestan. These Karakhanids (an inaccurate name given them in the 19th century) were the first truly Islamic Turkish dynasty and from their eastern capital of Kashgar they clashed with the Buddhist Uigurs and Khotanese. Their own civilization was built on Buddhist and Manichean as well as Islamic foundations. This exotic realm then passed such eastern cultural influences to the Muslim heartlands, via a Turkish warrior class which was rapidly dominating Middle Eastern armies. The first truly Turkish literature also appeared under the Karakhanids.

The Karakhanid empire consisted of a series of autonomous military fiefs on each side of the Tien-Shan. Their army remained a tribal force under tribal leaders, never including many professional *ghulams* or *mamluks* of slave origin as did most medieval Muslim forces. Loose central control at first led to a revival of the native military aristocracy of Transoxania and to the development of an almost feudal system of *iqta* military fiefs throughout the Karakhanid state. In other respects old habits continued in new guises. Tribes would now gather around mosques rather than a chieftain's *ordu* or camp. Fortified frontier *ribats*, garrisoned by religious volunteers, may have owed much to fortified Buddhist monasteries and great castles like that at Atbas still remain among the Karakhanids' most enduring monuments. Karakhanid warriors were described by a Muslim writer in AD 1008 as having 'broad faces, small eyes, flat

Central Asia (4th-6th C)
1: Hsiung-Nu warrior
2: Tashtyk tribesman
3: Kushan nobleman

A

The Huns in Europe (5th C)
1: Attila
2: Goth warrior of southern Russia
3: Bosphoran soldier

B

The Toba (5th-6th C)
1: Toba nobleman
2: Toba horseman
3: Chinese infantryman

C

The Eastern Huns (6th-8th C)
1: Hepthalite nobleman
2: Sughdian warrior
3: East Sassanian warrior

D

Avars and Bulgars (6th-8th C)
1: Avar nobleman
2: Balkan Bulgar warrior
3: Southern Slav warrior

E

The Turks (6th–8th C)
1: Türgish 'tarkan' champion
2: Gök 'Blue' Turk armoured cavalryman
3: Eastern Turk tribesman

F

The Uighurs (8th–9th C)
1: Uighur prince
2: Uighur heavy cavalryman
3: Sughdian merchant

G

The Khazar Khaganate (7th-10th C)
1: Alan nobleman
2: Khazar cavalryman
3: Muslim mercenary from Khwarazm

H

The Khirgiz (8th-9th C)
1: Khirgiz warrior
2: Kimak tribal warrior
3: Khirgiz tribesman

I

The Finno-Ugrians (11th–12th C)
1: Muroma (Finn) princess
2: Mordva (Finn) warrior
3: Ob-Ugrian tribesman

J

The Karakhitai Empire (11th–12th C)
1: Mongol tribal chief
2: Naiman warrior
3: Karakhitai nobleman

K

The western steppes (10th-13th C)
1: Volga Bulgar cavalryman
2: Kipchaq warrior
3: Pecheneg lady

L

noses, sparse beards, iron swords and black clothing'. Their equipment may be reflected in a number of battered chess-pieces found in Transoxania and, in the last years of Karakhanid power, some provincial armies still included non-Muslim warriors.

The Third Wave

Russian attacks on the Khazars weakened that long-enduring state but it is an oversimplification to say that they opened the way for further fierce nomads to pour into the western steppes. Yet a third wave of nomads, the Pechenegs, did emerge from their ancestral grazing grounds between the Volga River and Ural Mountains to occupy the Black Sea steppes in the 9th century. They were even more mixed than most tribal groups and though they spoke Turkish they included many Finno-Ugrians and people of Iranian nomad origin. Russians had been advancing into the steppes for generations but now their settlements and forts were devastated. Pechenegs may also have seized the grazing lands of Wallachia north of the Danube around the same time, though this is debatable as the Byzantines seem to have dominated both banks for much of the 10th century. Pechenegs certainly controlled central Moldavia; the Slav population of the lowlands being virtually obliterated. Nomads also pushed into the valleys of the southern Carpathians and settled the north bank of the Danube in the 11th century. Pushed by yet more hordes to the east, some Pechenegs fled into Hungary where they retained a separate identity for more than a century.

Meanwhile the Byzantine authorities seem to have encouraged other Pechenegs to settle along their Danube frontier as *feoderati* but in the mid-11th century these Pechenegs of the lower Danube turned upon their Byzantine hosts, only to be hit by disease and defeated in battle. The Byzantines tried to settle them in mountains unsuited to their nomadic ways but the tribesmen simply migrated back to the Danube plain where they became a local military aristocracy under nominal Byzantine control. Elsewhere the Pechenegs gradually merged with other peoples, including nomads such

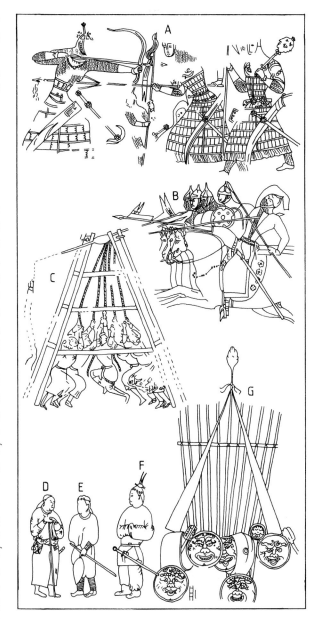

Wall-paintings from palace of Piandjikent, Transoxania, 7th–8th C. (Hermitage Mus., Leningrad): A—combat on foot, note similarity with combat on silver dish from Kulagysh; B—cavalry combat; C—one of the earliest representations of a man-powered mangonel; D—Gök Turk figure; E—visitor from Tashkent; F—warrior of Tudan dynasty; G—standards, flags and war-drums.

as the Torks and Kipchaqs (see below). It has also been suggested that the Turks who still inhabit the Dobruja of eastern Romania are descended from Pechenegs and Kipchaqs rather than later Ottoman settlers.

Militarily the Pechenegs remained a loose association of clans or families. Their leading tribe

'The Abduction of Lady Wen-Chi,' painted Chinese hand-scroll of *Eighteen Songs of a Nomad Flute*. This 14th century copy is a replica of the 8th century original. The invading nomads wear lamellar cuirasses and are armed with bows, clubs and straight swords while their mounts have two different forms of horse-armour. (Metropolitan Mus., Dillon Fund 1973.120.3, New York)

may have been descended from refugees who fled the Muslim conquest of Transoxania and their religious beliefs appear to have been a mixture of Iranian Zoroastrianism and Manicheism. The Pechenegs did not build many fortifications, preferring to obliterate the Russian castles which they overran. On the other hand the later Pechenegs who served as Byzantium's troublesome *feoderati* clearly used existing local citadels. In war the Pechenegs sold prisoners for ransom, this being a major source of income. They were described as clean-shaven and wearing relatively short tunics. Their great ox-headed bugles seem to echo those used earlier in Transoxania while their main weapons were, of course, the composite bow and the curved sabre. Byzantine chroniclers point to the great numbers of Pechenegs but also to their 'primitive' shortage of arms and armour. On the other hand possibly Pecheneg graves in southern Russia contain short-sleeved mail hauberks, tall helmets and anthropomorphic bronze visors. Islamic sources describe Pecheneg armies as small, compared to those of Byzantium, their tactics

including cavalry and infantry. The former held the wings and would make repeated circular archery attacks on the Byzantines before the whole Pecheneg army, including infantry at the centre, advanced to finish off their foes.

Before the fearsome Kipchaqs erupted into the western steppes other smaller Turkish nomad tribes had arrived in the wake of the Pechenegs. Among these were the Uzes or Torks who were an offshoot of the widespread Oghuz people. They also seem to have been related to the Pechenegs. In earlier centuries, along the north-eastern frontier of Iran, the Oghuz were clearly very Iranian in both costume and culture. Like the Pechenegs some were clean-shaven though others sported small 'goatee' beards. Like the Kimaks they set up many carved wooden funerary statues surrounded by simple stone *balbal* monoliths, while those along the Islamic frontier had become Muslim by the late 10th century. That part of the Oghuz people known as Uzes were then pushed westward by the Kipchaqs, in turn taking the western steppes from the Pechenegs. Their hold on these lands was, however, short-lived for they were soon scattered by the Kipchaqs who came close on their heels. Those Uzes or Torks who settled along the Russian frontier were gradually Slavized though they also played a leading rôle as cavalry in 12th and early 13th century Russian armies where they were known as 'Black Hats'. Others fled southwards and entered Byzantine service.

Brief as their history in eastern Europe was, the Oghuz had a very distinctive culture. Their hunting and banqueting rituals were as elaborate as those of the Gök Turks from whom they were inherited. The Oghuz epic national poem, *'The Book of Dede Korkut'*, was not written down until the 14th century but it remains one of very few Central Asian Turkish epics to have been translated into English. Oghuz warriors served in almost all Islamic armies of the Middle East from the 11th century onwards, in Byzantium from the 9th century, and even in Spain and Morocco.

The Berendei were another small people of Turkish origin who may have separated from the Oghuz or might have been more closely related to the Kipchaqs. They are mentioned in Russian chronicles from the late 11th century and, like some Pechenegs and Torks, settled along Russia's steppe frontier after being forced out by the Kipchaqs. Others fled into Hungary. It was in Russia, however, that these Berendei played their most significant role, providing many cavalrymen to the princes of Kiev and Pereiaslav on the lower Dnepr River. Here an almost feudal 'Black Hat' principality grew up with its own military aristocracy being accepted by the Russian elite on equal terms.

Peoples of the Forest

Along the northern edge of the great Eurasian steppe stand the even more extensive forests of Russia and Siberia. Their inhabitants included peoples of Turco-Mongol, Finno-Ugrian and Slav speech, not to mention the Tungus, Yakut and other more primitive Altaic people of north-eastern Siberia. Further north still lay the almost treeless frozen tundra bordering the Arctic Ocean. Until the expansion of the Russian Empire in the 16th and 17th centuries, the peoples of Siberia generally looked south to the steppes and beyond for their few contacts with the outside world. Nor were they as isolated as one might think. Furs, along with wood, fish and other products were exported via the Russian principalities or through

various settled or semi-nomadic Turkish states.

Trade was vital to the very existence of some peoples on or near the frontier between steppe and forest. This was certainly true of the Volga Bulgars who had migrated northward after the collapse of Old Bulgaria in the 7th century. They colonized a large area around the upper Volga and Kama Rivers, subjugating the local Finno-Ugrian tribes and creating a sophisticated trading community. These Bulgars brought with them a fully developed political, social and military system though at first they remained under the distant suzerainty of the Khazars. But in the early 10th century they threw off the Khazar yoke, looked to the Caliphate of Baghdad for assistance and as a result soon became Muslim. Their ruler adopted the Arabic title of *amir* and the Volga Bulgars sent missionaries to Kiev, to compete with Jews from Khazaria and Christians from Byzantium for the souls of Russia. They fought off Kipchaq attacks, numerous inva-

'Guardian of the North crushing a demon'; Buddhist statue at Dandan-Uilik, probably late 8th century Khotanese. The upper and lower parts of the armour differ though both probably represent lamellar. Such styles are closer to Transoxania and northern India than to China. (Aurel Stein)

sions by Russian princes who wanted to dominate the rich trading routes through Bulgar territory and, for a while, even kept the Mongols at bay. Though they lost their name after finally falling to the Mongols, the Turkish people remained and only fell to Russian artillery in AD 1552. Like the neighbouring Finno-Ugrians many converted to Christianity but a large Muslim population survives in the area to this day.

The Volga Bulgar state was a loose association of tribes and peoples in which local chieftains enjoyed effective independence under the *amir*'s suzerainty. Cities like Bulgar the Great numbered up to 50,000 inhabitants while five hundred leading families provided most of the military elite. The Volga Bulgars were, of course, no longer nomads but had taken to trading, fishing, cattle raising and agriculture along the river banks and in forest clearings. Leather goods were made for export. Swords, arrows and armour were locally manufactured and added to those in transit from Europe to the Muslim world and vice versa. Most buildings were still of wood and even the ruler lived in a tent during summer. Nevertheless the ambassadors from Baghdad brought skilled architects to help the Volga Bulgars build fortresses and castles of wood and earth. By the 13th century a few stone fortifications also seem to have appeared. In fact the Volga Bulgars seemed adept at defensive warfare from fixed positions, numerous spiked caltrops to cripple an enemy's horses having been found in a number of Bulgar sites. This is all a far cry from the traditionally fast-moving mounted warfare of the nomad Huns, Turks or Mongols.

Among the Volga Bulgars' forest neighbours was another Turkish-speaking people—the Bashkirs. They too had mixed origins; the name Bashkir sometimes also including those Magyars or Hungarians who had earlier remained in the Ural region rather than migrating to Hungary. The true Turkish Bashkirs lived near the steppe frontier south of the Volga Bulgars while the Magyar or Finno-Ugrian Bashkirs lived under Volga Bulgar rule deeper in the Ural forests. There, according to contemporary chronicles, they were 'protected by impassable thickets'. Most Bashkirs were also

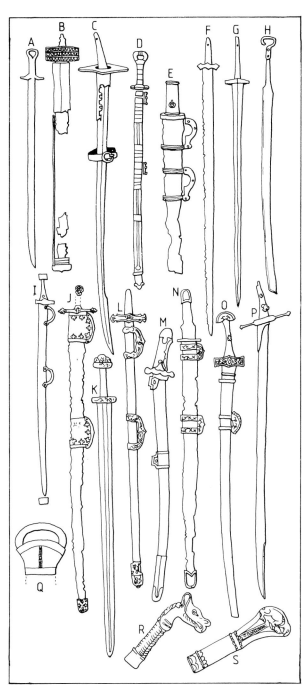

Swords: A—from Ural Mountains, 1st–5th C. (ex-Khudyakov); **B**—Hun from Altlussheim, Germany, 4th C. (location unknown); **C**—Turkish from Altai Mountains, 6th–10th C. (ex-Pletnyeva); **D**—from western steppes, 6th–7th C. (ex-Pletnyeva); **E**—Alan style but from Avar grave at Törökbálint, Hungary, early 7th C. (ex-Kovrig Ilona); **F**—Avar, 7th C. (Milit. Mus., Budapest); **G**—Kirghiz, 6th–9th C. (ex-Khudyakov); **H**—Ugrian from western Siberia, 6th–7th C. (ex-Solovyev); **I**—Volga Bulgar, 8th–10th C. (ex-Pletnyeva); **J**—Turkish or Iranian from Nishapur, 9th–10th C. (Met. Mus., New York); **K**—European import to Ugrian western Siberia, 10th–11th C. (ex-Sedov); **L**—Kimak, 9th–10th C. (ex-Khudyakov); **M**—from northern Caucasus, 9th C. (ex-Pletnyeva); **N**—Kimak or Qarluq, 9th–10th C. (ex-Pletnyeva); **O-P**—Kirghiz, 10th–12th C. (ex-Khudyakov); **Q**—Avar swordpommel from Kecel, 7th–8th C. (ex-Laszlo); **R-S**—cast bronze sword or dagger-hilts, Ugrian western Siberia, 7th–13th C. (ex-Sedov)

48

Muslim, including those who went to Hungary in the 12th century where they served against the Hungarian king's non-Muslim foes.

North and east of the Bashkirs lived various Ugrian tribes centred around the inhospitable, marshy and forested Ob river basin. Linguistically they were related to the Finns who still inhabited most of the forests of what is now European Russia (excluding White Russia and the Ukraine). Nevertheless these Ugrians remain a mysterious people.

Painted wooden panel from a Buddhist sanctuary, Dandan-Uilik, 7th–8th century. Here a horseman and camel-rider both carry long single-edged swords and use stirrups. (British Mus., London)

Their history is virtually unknown before the 11th century when Russian merchants from Novgorod started to penetrate their territory. In Russian legend the Ugrians appear as an inherently evil race who had been locked behind mythical Iron or Copper Gates by Alexander the Great and would only be released on Judgement Day. In reality the Ugrians had wide trading contacts to the south, undertaken by 'dumb barter' with the Volga Bulgars and others who could not understand their language.

Ugrian peoples of the far northern Urals may not have been warlike but other tribes had a reputation for savagery, once swallowing an entire army sent from Russian Novgorod under Prince Gleb in AD 1079. Some 12th century Russian expeditions into Ugrian territory were more successful, though others failed. Tribesmen of these far northern regions apparently used so-called flat bows of simple construction which were able to cope with the extreme cold. Elsewhere Ugrians used a characteristic form of sabre with a ring-like pommel formed by bending the hilt's exceptionally long tang. Other Ugrian weaponry, like their horse-harness, showed strong connections with steppe peoples to the south. Even swords of medieval Armenian and Central European origin have been found in Ugrian territory. From the 12th to 15th centuries, however, the Ugrians were gradually forced eastwards by advancing Russians and by Finns who were themselves being pushed by the Russians.

The Fourth Wave

Even before the rise of the Mongols, peoples whose cultures had their roots in China returned to the offensive against the essentially 'Western' civilizations of Islam and Christianity. The flourishing Muslim states of Central Asia were the first to feel this 'Far Eastern' revival though the Russians did not have long to wait.

Almost untouched by the cultural changes of the past few centuries, the Turkish-speaking Kirghiz had wandered the steppes of the upper Yenisi River north of Mongolia. Isolated behind the Sayan mountains the Kirghiz had nevertheless developed a rich metal-working tradition and appear to have owned abundant weapons. Some of their ruling elite were described as red haired, blue or green eyed, white skinned and were probably descended from ancient Indo-European peoples. The bulk of Kirghiz tribesmen were, however, Turco-Mongol. From this obscurity they suddenly emerged in AD 840 to overthrow the Uighur empire and for the next eighty-four years ruled their own brief empire in eastern Turkestan. But then the Kirghiz were themselves defeated by the Khitai, a people of strongly Chinese culture, being thrust back into their original homeland north of the mountains where they fell under Genghis Khan's domination in the early 13th century. Christianity had spread among the Kirghiz but most remained pagan until gradually converting to Islam in the 16th century.

Much more significant were the Karakhitai ('Black' Khitai), descended from the same Mongol Khitai whose domination over northern China was overthrown by the Kin in AD 1125. The Kin or Chin would in turn be destroyed by Genghis Khan's Mongols early in the 13th century. Meanwhile 16,000 Khitai families migrated west with their livestock to join fellow Khitai already in eastern Turkestan. There they built the new Karakhitai state. Previous Khitai attacks on the Muslim Karakhanids had failed but now the fragmented Karakhanid state collapsed, the provincial governor of Balasaghun south of Lake Balkash being the first Muslim ruler to submit to these conquering 'infidels'. Later Karakhitai victories over the Seljuqs in Transoxania probably gave rise to new legends about Prester John among European Crusaders who were then alarmed at a revival of Muslim unity in the Middle East. This Prester John was seen as a Christian monarch of unlimited power who would attack the Muslims from the rear and join with the Crusaders to destroy Islam for ever. In reality the first *Gurkhan* of the Karakhitai was probably a Manichean rather than a Christian while most of his followers were Buddhists or pagan shamanists. Yet there is no doubt that the Karakhitai persecuted Muslims with vigour, prompting a Muslim revolt in the late 12th and early 13th centuries. Remarkable as it may seem, Genghis Khan was actually seen as a liberator by the Muslims of eastern Turkestan when he overthrew the Karakhitai! Karakhitai

'Uighurs paying homage to Chinese general Guo Zui', Chinese hand-scroll by Li Gonglin, 11th-12th century. Many details of later Uighur military fashion, like feathered crests on the horses' chamfrons, hark back to crude Central Asian rock-pictures while others, like the warriors' arm defences, foreshadow 15th century Timurid art from eastern Iran. (National Palace Mus., Taiwan)

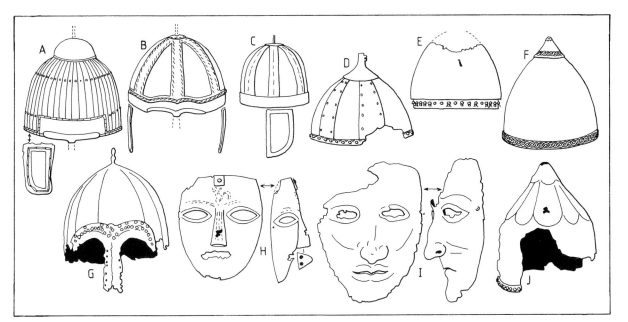

persecution of Islam also led to a strong backlash which eventually resulted in the virtual disappearance of Buddhism, Manicheism and Christianity in Central Asia and their replacement by Islam as far as the Chinese border.

The Karakhitai state looked to China for military as well as cultural inspiration. In this they differed from previous nomad empires and had more in common with the subsequent Mongols. They could even be described as the 'vanguard' of the Mongol flood which soon submerged so much of Asia. Some Karakhitai rulers veiled their faces and were regarded as semi-divine. They and their leading aristocracy wore Chinese silks while local rulers who accepted Karakhitai suzerainty were given silver belts as a badge of homage. All males from the age of eighteen served in the army and the Karakhitai state was organized along feudal rather than tribal lines. The little that is known about the Karakhitai army suggests that it again included large numbers of infantry and that its weaponry reflected Chinese influence.

North and east of the Karakhitai lived the true Mongols, some of whom accepted the Karakhitai *Gurkhan*'s nominal authority. Among the most advanced of these relatively primitive people was the Naiman tribal confederation. Its leader Kuchlug actually defeated the last Karakhitai ruler and in AD 1211 proclaimed his own empire stretching from eastern Mongolia to Khotan in the south, Farghana in the west and Lake Balkash in

the north. However, it proved to be the briefest such Central Asian state, being destroyed by Genghis Khan only eight years later. The Mongols had, in fact, already made several attempts to unify their disparate tribes. Nor were they as backward or as unknown as some still suggest. Genghis was himself a great-nephew of the last Khan of the tribes which had dominated what is now eastern Mongolia in the early 12th century. But these Mongols had been defeated by their hereditary Tatar foes, remaining disorganized and almost leaderless until the rise of Genghis Khan.

Far to the west another Central Asian people was also shattering the existing framework and paving the way for the Mongols. These were the Turkish-speaking Kipchaqs. In Russia they were known as Polovtsi, in Byzantium as Chomanoi or Sauromates and in Central Europe as Coumans or Kun—these names meaning steppe dweller. At one time the Kipchaqs were thought to have been fair skinned and almost European in appearance but recent archaeological studies have indicated that the majority of Kipchaqs were Turco-

Mongol. The fact that they were also regarded as a handsome people, noted for the beauty of their women, shows how far east European perceptions of Asiatic peoples had changed since the Romans with their detestation of the 'hideous' Huns.

Stemming from the Kimaks and with a material culture similar to that of the Pechenegs, these Kipchaqs drove the Oghuz from the south Russian steppes which they then held until the coming of the Mongols over a century and a half later. They dominated the coastal towns of the northern Black Sea and ruled over various Slav, Finno-Ugrian and Iranian nomad peoples. From their bases in Wallachia and Moldavia the Kipchaqs raided across the Danube deep inside Byzantine territory, sometimes allying themselves with the Normans of southern Italy or the Hungarians who attacked Byzantium from the west. After AD 1159 the Kipchaqs shifted their main centre north to the Dnepr River from which they raided Russia, though some remained to be assimilated by the Romanian-speaking Vlachs of the Carpathians.

Kipchaq families were headed by *begs*, these families themselves forming *hordes* under the rule of *sultans*. Several hordes formed a tribe ruled by a *khan*. All able-bodied men were still expected to serve in the army although the Kipchaqs were also noted for their warrior women. This social structure nevertheless gradually gave way to an almost feudal system and, by the 12th century, the Kipchaqs were fast abandoning their nomadic ways. Many settled down to agriculture and crafts such as iron or leather working, saddle-making and bow-making—trades which reflected their steppe traditions. Kipchaq towns grew up in Moldavia and Kipchaq merchants travelled the ancient trade routes from eastern Europe to the Middle East. Almost to the end, however, the largely pagan tribesmen in the east of the Kipchaq state were still carving elaborate stone statues of warriors and ladies to be placed on the tombs of important people.

Although the warlike Kipchaqs were often in conflict with their neighbours, they also formed alliances with Byzantines, Georgians and others. Kipchaq warriors served in various Russian princely armies and Christianity, as well as Islam, was spreading fast by the early 13th century. Daughters of the Kipchaq military elite were

marrying into the Russian aristocracy and, in fact, it looked as if this once fierce people would soon be assimilated into the medieval European world. To their north the leading Russian principality of Kiev was in decline although in the western Ukraine the principality of Galich was growing in power. On the far side of the Danube Kipchaqs had settled in Byzantine territory, first as garrisons and then as a fief or *pronoia*-holding military aristocracy. These men appear to have played a major rôle in the rise of the so-called Second Bulgarian Empire at the very end of the 12th century.

The military organization of the Kipchaqs naturally developed over these years and though their army was large it was, as usual, greatly exaggerated by its non-nomadic foes. According to the Byzantine historian Nicetas the early nomadic Kipchaqs fought with a quiver on their hip, a recurve bow, javelins and a curved sabre. They used the traditional Turkish tactics of repeated charges by horse-archers, feigned flight and skilful ambush. According to the Crusader Robert de

The wall-paintings uncovered in the pre-Islamic palace of Piandjikent, not far from Samarkand, illustrate battles, hunting, feasting and religious celebration. Helmets are almost always very pointed with cheek-pieces and mail aventails, some pulled over the wearer's face. Warriors wear long or short-sleeved mail hauberks, some alone, others under tunics or lamellar cuirasses. Bows are carried unstrung in long cases, swords are straight and round shields are small while a distinctive form of horse-bit curves around the front of the animal's mouth. Many such features were adopted by the Muslim armies which conquered Transoxania shortly after these pictures were painted. (Hermitage Mus., Leningrad)

Clari the ordinary tribesmen dressed in sheep-skins and had ten or twelve horses.

By the later years the Kipchaqs also fielded heavily armoured cavalrymen as well as lightly equipped horse-archers. It was also possible for the far less mobile Russians to surprise a Kipchaq army in camp, which suggests that their speed was reduced by relatively slow baggage waggons. These would in any case have been needed to carry the Kipchaqs' sophisticated incendiary weapons, mangonels and other siege equipment which they used against Russia's wooden fortifications. Some Kipchaq waggons were also armed with crossbows, perhaps of the large frame-mounted type used in Byzantium and the Muslim world. In the Balkans Kipchaq armies were often accompanied by local Vlach tribesmen, most of whom would have fought as infantry (see MAA 195 *Hungary and the Fall of Eastern Europe*). Meanwhile topographical and archaeological evidence shows that the Kipchaqs built many forts as well as other settlements in the lowlands of what is now eastern and southern Romania.

Then sudden disaster struck as Mongol hordes poured into the Russian steppes from the east. Once again nomadism triumphed and the slow advance of urbanization, settled agriculture and European Christianity was reversed for another century. Many Kipchaqs were absorbed into the Mongol armies and soon came to dominate the Golden Horde which emerged from the fragmentation of the Mongol World Empire. Others fled into the Carpathian valleys and appear to have provided the first ruling dynasty of an independent 'Romanian' Wallachia which emerged a century later.

Further reading

V. V. Barthold, trans. V. and T. Minorsky, *Four Studies on the History of Central Asia, vol. I: A Short History of Turkestan; and History of Semirechye* (Leiden 1962)

R. Browning, *Byzantium and Bulgaria: A Comparative Study across the early medieval frontier* (London 1975)

P. Diaconu, *Les Coumans au Bas-Danube aux XIe au XIIe siècles* (Bucharest 1978)

P. Diaconu, *Les Petchénègues au Bas-Danube* (Bucharest 1970)

W. Eberhard, *Das Toba-Reich Nordchinas* (Leiden 1949)

Encyclopedia of Islam, 2nd edit. (Leiden 1960 continuing)

E. Esin, *A History of Pre-Islamic and Early Islamic Turkish Culture* (Istanbul 1980)

Great Soviet Encyclopedia, trans. of 13th edit. (London 1977)

R. Grousset, trans. N. Walford, *The Empire of the Steppes: A History of Central Asia* (New Brunswick 1970)

O. Lattimore, 'Inner Asian Frontiers: Defensive Empires and Conquest Empires', in *Studies in Frontier History* (London 1962)

R. P. Lindner, 'Nomadism, Horses and Huns', *Past and Present* XCII (1981) pp. 3–19

C. Mackerras, *The Uighur Empire according to the T'ang Dynastic Histories* (Canberra 1972)

O. Maenchen-Helfen, *The World of the Huns* (London 1973)

H. Nickl, 'About the Sword of the Huns and the "Urepos" of the Steppes', *Metropolitan Museum Journal* VII (1973) pp. 131–42

H. Paszkiewicz, *The Origin of Russia* (London 1954)

K. M. Setton, 'The Bulgars in the Balkans and the Occupation of Corinth in the Seventh Century', *Speculum* XXV (1950) pp. 502–43

D. Sinor, 'Horse and Pasture in Inner Asian History', *Oriens Extremus* XIX (1972) pp. 171–84

D. Sinor, 'The Inner Asian Warriors', *Journal of the American Oriental Society* CI (1981) pp. 133–44

A. Stein, *On Ancient Central Asian Tracks* (London 1933)

R. E. Sullivan, 'Khan Boris and the Conversion of Bulgaria', *Studies in Medieval and Renaissance History* III (1966) pp. 55–139

E. A. Thompson, *A History of Attila and the Huns* (Oxford 1948)

E. Yarshater, edit., *The Cambridge History of Iran, vol. 3/1: The Seleucid, Parthian and Sassanian Periods* (Cambridge 1983)

Armour like that of Piandjikent also appears on a painted shield from the castle of Mug. This early 8th century shield dates from a war-torn period when Arabs, Chinese and Turks struggled for control of Central Asia. (Hermitage Mus., Leningrad)

The Plates

A: Central Asia, 4th–6th centuries:

A1: Hsiung-Nu warrior, 4th century

This warrior wears a bronze lamellar helmet and neck protection, and a high-collared quilted tunic beneath a simple leather lamellar cuirass. Such defences appear in a lot of variously dated Central Asian art. Bronze lamellae also protect his legs, while his sword is suspended by a scabbard-slide of the type used before the introduction of the twin-strap system associated with the single-edged sabre. Note that he has no stirrups. (Main sources: 6th C. sword-belt from Sayan-Altai Mts., ex-Pletnyeva; 6th C. sword from Kirghiz area, ex-Khudyakov; leather lamellae from Niya, 3rd C., Brit. Mus.; Buddhist temple paintings from Kizil valley and Tumsuk, 5th–6th C., Staat. Mus., West Berlin.)

A2: Tashtyk tribesman, 4th–5th centuries

The most characteristic feature of Tashtyk military equipment was an enormous rectangular shield which is normally shown on a man's back in Tashtyk art. Such shields were probably of animal hide over a wooden frame. Some bows were of recurved shape but simple wooden construction; while an interesting south Siberian sword had its blade, quillons and pommel-ring forged from a single piece. (Main sources: incised wooden plank with hunting scene, Tashtyk, 3rd–4th C., Hermitage Mus.; south Siberian bow, 2nd–5th C., ex-Khudyakov.)

A3: Kushan nobleman, 4th–5th centuries

Kushan arms, armour and costume were influenced by India, Iran, China and Central Asia. This man's small turban was probably of Indian inspiration while his typically Kushan sword includes Chinese elements. The rest of his dress is east Iranian. He also uses a primitive form of 'loop stirrup'. (Main sources: 'Idol of Surya', late Kushan, 4th C., Kabul Mus.; Iranians on Indian wall painting, 5th C., *in situ* Ajanta; statues of Kushan rulers, 2nd C., Archaeol. Mus., Mathura; silver bowl, Kushan, Brit. Mus.; engraved copper cup from Taxila, Kushan, 1st–2nd C., Brit. Mus.)

B: Attila and the Huns in Europe, 5th century:
B1: Attila, c.AD 450

It is not known whether or not the Huns continued to dress in Central Asian style after settling in Europe. Nevertheless, Attila has here been given the kind of fur-lined hat, long coat, baggy trousers and soft boots worn by Huns and other nomads further east. His bow-case is for two unstrung weapons, while his quiver is slung across his back as appears in crude eastern Hun art. Attila's gilded

The mountains between China and the Soviet Union, between eastern and western Turkestan, are dotted with castles though few have been studied. Many are known locally as Kafir or 'infidel' citadels, suggesting a pre-Islamic origin. This, at Zamr-i-Atish Parast in the Pamir mountains, is built of stone in an Iranian style different from the Chinese military architecture of eastern Turkestan. (Aurel Stein)

sword with its lapis lazuli guard and jade scabbard-slide is a princely weapon, and his decorated saddle and harness are also shown as being of high quality. Note that the saddle is padded rather than wood-framed. Attila also carries a symbolic gold-covered bow. (Main sources: incised Hun metalwork, ex-Khudyakov; gilded Hun bow from Jakuszowice, location unknown; clothing from burial at Noin Ula, 1st C. BC–1st C. AD; weapons, belts, saddle and harness, ex-Pletnyeva and Werner.)

B2: Goth warrior of southern Russia, late 4th–early 5th centuries

Many of the Goths who remained to serve in Attila's armies had long been under the military influence of Sarmatian and Alan nomads. This accounted for their tall segmented helmets and long swords supported by scabbard-slides. This

Bronze strap-end from Klarafalva, Avar, 8th century. Once thought to be Magyar-Hungarian, this decorative piece of military belt shows the hunter-horseman who was a popular motif in the arts of Central Asia and Iran. He draws a reflex bow and has a large quiver of the enclosed box type. (Móra Ferenc Museum, Szeged)

warrior's costume is otherwise typically Germanic. (Main sources: Migration Period helmet from southern Russia, present location unknown; Goth sword from Taman, south Russia, ex-Oakeshott; Migration Period scabbard mounts from Romania, ex-Werner.)

B3: Soldier of the Bosphoran kingdom, early 5th century

The Greek-speaking Bosphorans of southern Russia had also been strongly influenced by their nomadic neighbours before the coming of the Huns. This soldier has a segmented helmet held together by rawhide thongs, an iron lamellar cuirass of a type used in very late Roman armies and a long sword showing clear Sassanian influence. The decoration around the top of his scabbard is, however, Germanic. (Main sources: helmet from Crimea, 5th C., location unknown; late Roman lamellar armour, Nat. Mus., Budapest; sword and scabbard, Russian steppes, Migration Period, ex-Werner.)

C: The Toba of northern China, 5th–6th centuries:
C1: Toba nobleman, 6th century

The costumes illustrated in Toba art are almost entirely Central Asian though their fabric is likely to have been Chinese. A coat opening down the front rather than having a wide double-breasted front is an early style betraying Sughdian influence. The man's dagger is a type known from northern China as far west as Transoxania while his thick-bladed sword, though suspended from the new form of doubled straps, is a very Chinese weapon. His saddle is of an early wood-framed type. (Main sources: carved funerary couch, northern Ch'i AD 550–577, Mus. Fine Arts, Boston; carved stele, western Toba AD 554, Mus. Fine Arts, Boston; wall painting from Kizil valley, 7th C., Staat. Mus., West Berlin.)

C2: Toba horseman, 5th century

Toba cavalry armour seems largely to have been of hardened leather. Note that this trooper's shoulder pieces are shown detached. The thickly padded neck protection was characteristic in this early period and the man's sword still incorporates a scabbard-slide. Both these Toba horsemen now use stirrups although this man's saddle is of the padded variety. (Main sources: tomb figures, northern Toba, 5th C., Brit. Mus. and Mus. Cernuschi, Paris; carved mortuary house, northern Toba, AD 527, Mus. Fine Arts, Boston.)

C3: Chinese infantryman in Toba service, 5th century

The large shields of northern Chinese infantry under nomad Toba rule are mirrored in Central Asia and may have been used by those Hun warriors who 'leaned upon their shields' in Europe. The armour made of overlapping sheets of rawhide used by this infantryman was cheap but presumably effective. The oval pieces on his chest gave shape to the body armour. (Main sources: tomb figures, northern Toba and other minor dynasties, 5th–6th C., Brit. Mus. and Royal Ontario Mus.; carved mortuary house, northern Toba, AD 527, Mus. Fine Arts, Boston.)

D: The Eastern Huns, 6th–8th centuries:

D1: Hephthalite nobleman, 7th century

The aristocracy of pre-Islamic Transoxania wore magnificent clothes and jewellery. Here a member of the ruling elite retains the plaited hair of the steppe warrior but is otherwise dressed in Iranian style. From his belt hang a purse and kerchief as well as a narrow-bladed dagger and a long straight sword with a ring-pommel more normally associated with the people of the northern steppes and forests. (Main sources: sword, scabbard, belt-mounts and jewellery from Transoxania and the central steppes, ex-Pletnyeva; wall paintings from Piandjikent palace, 7th–8th C., Hermitage Mus.)

D2: Sughdian warrior, early 8th century

Many styles of military costume and equipment are illustrated on the Piandjikent wall-paintings, this figure being based upon some of the simpler. His mixed iron and hardened leather segmented helmet has a full aventail drawn up to the brow while beneath his tunic he wears a mid-sleeved, mail hauberk. In addition to the normal large dagger he also has a pen-case and a purse hanging from his belt. The heavy bronze mace is based upon an object that might equally, however, have been a piece of furniture decoration. (Main sources: spiked bronze 'object' from Turkestan, present location unknown; wall-paintings from Piandjikent, 7th–8th C., Hermitage Mus.; Iranian helmet from Oskol, 8th–9th C., Hermitage Mus.)

D3: East Sassanian warrior, 7th–8th century

The warrior elite of what is now Afghanistan were equipped in a basically Central Asian manner but dressed in more Iranian fashions. This man's short mail hauberk is worn beneath a tight-fitting tunic. Around his legs are decorated leather gaiters rather than the floppy boots of the nomads and his dagger is smaller than those seen among Turkish peoples. His sword is a transitional form between the Sassanian long sword and the Central Asian proto-sabre. (Main sources: Sassanian dagger, 6th–7th C., Met. Mus., New York; Sassanian or

Graffiti and other incised decorations: A—petraglyph, Hsiung-Nu, 1st–4th C. (*in situ* Cagaan Gol, Mongolia); B—Hun decoration, 2nd–5th C. (ex-Khudyakov); C—graffiti of Kokel people, southern Siberia, 2nd–5th C. (ex-Khudyakov); D—incised wooden plank from Tashtyk burial, 3rd C. (Hermitage Mus., Leningrad); E—Bulgar graffiti from Preslav fortress, 8th–10th C. (location unknown); F—decoration on Turkish bowcase from Upper Khir-Yurt, northern Caucasus, 7th–8th C. (ex-Pletnyeva); G—petraglyphs, east Turkish, **6th–7th C. (*in situ* Char-chad, Mongolia); H-I—on incised metal plaque from Siberia, poss 8th–10th C. (ex-Medvedyev); J—later incised decoration on Khazar silver dish from Siberia, poss 8th–10th C. (ex-Medvedyev); K—Khazar graffiti from north-east of Sea of Azov, 9th–10th C. (location unknown); L-M—Kirghiz petraglyphs, 9th–10th C. (ex-Khudyakov); N-O—Kirghiz petraglyphs, 11th–12th C. (ex-Khudyakov)**

post-Sassanian swords, 6th–7th C., Brit. Mus., Met. Mus., Tenri Sankokan Mus., Tokyo; wall-painting from Buddhist monastery in Fundikistan, 6th–7th C., Archaeol. Mus., Kabul; 'hunting scene' on rock relief, 7th–8th C., *in situ* Taq-i-Bustan, Iran.)

E: Avars and Bulgars, 6th–8th centuries:

E1: Avar nobleman, 7th–8th century

The Avars appear to have retained many Asian styles when they entered Europe though they had abandoned nomadism. This man has the pendant belt associated with a Central Asian military elite, a quiver that almost entirely encloses his arrows and a bow kept unstrung in a bowcase with a hinged end. His straight sword is an elaborate version of the ring-pommel type but his helmet is European, having been captured in Central Europe. His saddle is of the fully developed wood-framed form and he uses proper stirrups. (Main sources: helmet from Prag-Stromovka, Nat. Mus., Prague; all other aspects of costume, weaponry and harness, ex-Laszlo.)

E2: Balkan Bulgar warrior, 6th–7th centuries

Less Bulgar military equipment has survived than Avar, but a few crude illustrated sources are available. Written descriptions also make it clear that the Balkan Bulgars soon adopted some Byzantine fashions, such as this man's tunic and trousers which reflect Byzantine military uniform. His helmet is a simple iron-framed leather spangenhelm. His short lamellar cuirass has a buff leather chest protection based upon that seen in Toba China while a true curved sabre hangs from his typical pendant belt. (Main sources: sword and belt, ex-Pletnyeva; inscribed tile from Madara, Bulgar, 7th C., location unknown; helmet from Bezirk Muras, late 6th–early 7th C., location unknown.)

E3: Southern Slav warrior, 6th century

Here a tribesman of southern Slav origin has been given a tattered ex-Byzantine military uniform, a captured Germanic helmet and an axe and javelins of probable Slav origin. (Main sources: south Slav saddle decorations from northern Greece, 7th C., ex-Werner; helmet from St. Vid, 6th–7th C., Archaeol. Mus., Split; axe from Butrint, Albania, 6th–8th C., ex-Anamali; javelins from Dalmatia, 6th–7th C., Mus. of Croat Arch., Split.)

Among the statues which dotted the steppes of southern Russia are some which were once thought to be Hun, though they are now known to be Pechenegs or Kipchaqs, probably from the 12th century. This example comes from Kerch in the Crimea, an area under Byzantine influence which would explain the pseudo-Roman elements in the armour. (State Historical Mus., Moscow)

F: The Turks, 6th–8th centuries:

F1: Türgish 'tarkan' champion, 7th century

Among warriors shown in the Piandjikent wall-paintings, one is so magnificently attired that he must either be a mythical hero or a *tarkan* champion, though his equipment is basically the same as that of other heavily armoured Transoxanian warriors. Even his 'lion's head' sleeves are seen in the art of eastern Turkestan and may be the reality behind the 'lion-skin cuirass' of the medieval Persian hero, Rustam. The man's weaponry consists of composite bows, a large dagger and a long straight sword with a particularly fine 'chip-carved' gilded bronze grip. (Main sources: helmet, belt, sword, scabbard and dagger from 7th–8th C. western steppes and southern Siberia, ex-Pletnyeva and Sedov; wall-painting from Piandji-kent, 7th–8th C., Hermitage Mus.)

F2: Gök 'Blue' Turk armoured cavalryman, 6th–7th centuries

Far more basic are the arms and armour of this horseman, though the twin feathers in his iron helmet show him to be a champion horse-archer. His cuirass is of hardened leather lamellae, each row being covered with a strip of fabric. The lamellae of the horse armour are uncovered. On his spear he carries one of the small bells beloved of Turkish warriors while his sword is still of the straight double-edged variety with substantial quillons. (Main sources: reconstruction by M. N. Gorelik based upon 6th–7th C. petraglyphs at Char Chad, Mongolia; sword, belt and spearhead 6th–7th C., ex-Pletnyeva; clay horse from Astana, 7th–8th C., Brit. Mus.)

F3: Eastern Turk tribesman, 7th century

Here an unarmoured tribesman draws blood from the neck of his horse, as Turks did for food in desperate circumstances. His long hair is typically Turkish but his tunic, wide trousers and soft boots were common steppe attire still being worn by the Mongols in the 13th century. His bowcase is for a strung weapon and has a fine tooled decoration. His stirrups, however, are of a simple leather 'loop'

The Turks' passion for large statues continued for some centuries after their conversion to Islam. This stucco figure dates from around AD 1200 and comes from western Iran. (Metropolitan Mus., Timken Burnett Fund 57.51.18, New York)

variety also used by poorer tribesmen well into the 14th century. (Main sources: decorated bowcases from Khir-Yurt and Altai mountains, Turkish, 6th–8th C., ex-Pletnyeva; carved fragment showing stirrup, 8th–9th C., Staat. Mus., West Berlin; bridle, dagger, belt and quiver, Turkish, 6th–8th C., ex-Pletnyeva.)

G: The Uighurs, 8th–9th centuries

G1: Uighur prince, 9th century

The precise meaning of this man's headgear is

unknown but it almost certainly indicated rank. The broad cummerbund beneath his belt would still be used by the Muslim Timurids in the 15th century while the bowcase and quiver are of fully developed medieval forms. Only the man's boots, held up by laces to an unseen belt, recall older fashions. (Main sources: sword from Sayan mountains, 10th C., ex-Khudyakov; Buddhist wall-paintings from Bezeklik, Uighur, 9th–10th C., Berlin, probably destroyed in WW2; Buddhist wall-painting from Turfan, Uighur, 9th–10th C., Staat. Mus., West Berlin.)

G2: Uighur heavy cavalryman, 9th century
Lamellar head protections seem to have persisted into the Uighur period. Here one is made from bronze lamellae on a thickly padded leather base. The rest of the man's armour is of hardened leather, some pieces also being laquered. (Main sources: sword from Sayan mountains, 10th C., ex-Khudyakov; lamellae from Miram, 8th–9th C., Brit. Mus.; painted paper fragment from Yar, Uighur, 9th C., Staat. Mus., West Berlin; statuette from Sorçuk, 8th C., Staat. Mus., West Berlin.)

G3: Sughdian merchant, 9th century
Merchants from many nations travelled the great Silk Road but Sughdians from Transoxania were among the most numerous. This man appears to have been trading in bales of 'horse-brasses' carried by his two-humped Bactrian camel. He is dressed in a mixture of Central Asian styles against the severe weather, plus his own Sughdian fashions and he is armed with an Iranian sabre hung from a Turkish sword-belt. (Main sources: sword from Nishapur, 9th–10th C., Met. Mus., New York; statuette of Muslim merchant, T'ang, 9th C., Royal Ontario Mus.; Buddhist wall-paintings from Bezeklik, Uighur, 9th–10th C., Berlin, probably destroyed in WW2.)

H: The Khazar Khaganate, 7th–10th centuries
H1: Alan nobleman, 8th century
Almost the complete costume of an Alan nobleman has been found in a grave in the northern Caucasus; other items of military equipment having been excavated at other sites. This figure is based on these finds which include a leather-lined cap or helmet with a metal finial, an Iranian-Islamic style

of kaftan coat, a fully curved and tapering sabre, a simply decorated leather bowcase with a composite bow and a particularly fine dagger with a silvered hilt and silver sheath. (Main sources: clothing and archery equipment from Moshchevaya Balka, 8th–9th C., Ethnog. Mus., Leningrad; belts and weapons from various Alan graves, 7th–9th C., ex-Pletnyeva.)

H2: Khazar cavalryman, 9th–10th centuries
Full mail hauberks of a type that would become common in 12th century Europe were used by Khazars as well as Byzantines and western Muslim troops. Here a heavily armoured cavalryman also has a helmet forged from a single piece of iron with a mail coif or more probably aventail plus splinted arm and leg defences similar to those found in early medieval Scandinavia. Only his slightly curved sabre puts him in a Turkish steppe tradition. (Main sources: gold ewer from Nagyszentmiklos Treasure, Caucasus, 7th–10th C., Kunsthist. Mus., Vienna; war-axe from southern Urals, 9th–10th C., ex-Mazhitov; helmet from southern Urals, Khazar-Bulgar, 10th–11th C., ex-Mazhitov; sword, belt and whip, western steppes, 9th–10th C., ex-Pletnyeva.)

H3: Muslim mercenary from Khwarazm, 9th–10th centuries
Written descriptions indicate that the Muslim troops who served as the Khazar ruler's bodyguard were equipped in Iranian-Islamic style. This man has a copper-covered iron helmet with a long mail aventail. Over a long-sleeved but short-hemmed mail hauberk he has the added protection of an iron lamellar cuirass while his broad straight sword is of Arab form with a bronze hilt from the area of Armenia. The gilded 'blade' on top of his banner is a standard rather than a weapon. (Main sources: wall-painting fragments from Nishapur, Iran, 10th C., Met. Mus., New York; sword-guard from al Rabadhah, Arabia, 7th–10th C., King Saud Univ. Mus., Riyadh; early Islamic helmet from Iraq, 7th–8th C., Brit. Mus.; bronze belt or harness decorations from Nishapur, Iran, 9th–11th C., Met. Mus., New York, and Archaeol. Mus., Tehran; ceramic dish from Nishapur, Iran, 9th–10th C., Mus. Orient. Art, Rome.)

I: The Kirghiz, 8th–9th centuries
I1: Kirghiz warrior, 8th century

Though isolated, the Kirghiz had advanced weaponry. This warrior's one-piece helmet is particularly fine. Apart from a thickly quilted coat his only other armour is a chest protection of overlapping iron lames. His highly decorated sword is, however, still of the straight double-edged type. (Main sources: helmet from Tomsk area, 7th–10th C., ex-Medvedyev; sword and scabbard from Altai Mts., Kirghiz, 7th–8th C., Hermitage Mus.; Buddhist wall-painting from Koço, 9th C., Staat. Mus., West Berlin; stucco horse from Ming-oi, 8th C., Brit. Mus.; Kirghiz armour, 6th–8th C., ex-Medvedyev.)

I2: Kimak tribal warrior, 9th century

The abundant weaponry found in pagan Kimak graves include types of armour mid-way between lamellar and scale. Some Kimak armour may have been imported from settled civilizations but this warrior's segmented helmet is typical of the medieval steppes and Russia. His bowcase again has tooled decoration portraying a horse-archer while his straight sword has the non-symmetrical quillons more commonly associated with sabres. (Main sources: Kimak sword, 9th–10th C., ex-Khudyakov; helmet from Legerevskie, 9th–10th C., ex-Mazhitov; Kimak armour, 9th–10th C., ex-Khudyakov.)

I3: Kirghiz tribesman, 9th century

Later Kirghiz military equipment showed greater Chinese influence. It also had much in common with that of the later Mongols. This heavily armoured cavalryman has armour almost entirely of iron lamellae, plus an iron helmet reinforced with iron bands. The beginnings of plate armour can be seen in his shoulder pieces and the disc over his chest which may have covered a lacing system. The laminated vambraces on his lower arms are in a long-established Transoxanian tradition while his shins would be protected by mail strips which appear, though not very clearly, in some Buddhist wall-paintings. The horse's armour is of leather lamellar with a flexible disc over the animal's shoulder to prevent chafing. (Main sources: Kirghiz sword, 9th–10th C., ex-Khudyakov; Kirghiz armour, 9th–12th C., ex-Khudyakov; Buddhist

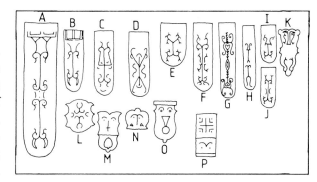

Tamgas or tribal marks, mostly on metal belt-ends: A–D—Avar from Kiskörös-Városalatt; E-L—Avar from Martinovka; M-N—Finno-Ugrian, early medieval; O—from Caucasus, early medieval; P—early medieval from Martinovka, Hungary.

wall-paintings from Bezeklik, 9th–10th C., Berlin, probably lost in WW2; Buddhist wall-painting from Kumtura, 8th C., Staat. Mus., West Berlin; painted paper fragment from Yar, Uighur, 9th C., Staat. Mus., West Berlin.)

J: The Finno-Ugrians, 11th–12th centuries
J1: Muroma (Finn) princess, 11th century

The wealth of some forest peoples north of the steppes is shown by the jewellery interred with their dead. Gold, like that worn by this lady of the Muroma people, inevitably attracted predatory neighbours from the steppes and from other parts of the forest zone. (Source: *Finno-Ugrians and Balts in the Middle Ages* by Sedov.)

J2: Mordva (Finn) warrior, 11th–12th centuries

Finno-Ugrian male graves are rarely as rich as those of some females. This tribal warrior has a typical Finn knife at his belt and is armed with a spear, a light javelin and an axe that could probably be thrown. His helmet was actually found in Baltic Prussia but is of a basic type found all over what is now European Russia. (Main sources: knife, sheath, axe, javelin and spear, 8th–12th C., ex-Sedov; helmet from Prussia, 9th–13th C., ex-Sedov.)

J3: Ob-Ugrian tribesman, 10th–11th centuries

Only recently have the archaeological remains of the Ugrian tribes east of the Ural Mountains been fully studied. This man is armed with a sword that somehow found its way from western Europe or Scandinavia. Beneath his saddle he also carries a simple sabre with a variation on the ring-pommel seen in many parts of the central steppes and Siberian forests. Beneath his heavy fur coat he wears a simple form of rawhide lamellar cuirass. (Main sources: European-type sword, horse-harness and belt fragments, Ugrian, 6th–13th C., ex-Sedov; leather lamellae, undated west Siberian, ex-Solovyev; bronze statuette or harness decoration, west Siberian, 6th–13th C., ex-Solovyev; sabre, west Siberian, 11th–14th C., ex-Solovyev.)

K: The Karakhitai Empire, 11th–12th centuries
K1: Mongol tribal chief, 11th century

Although the early Mongols had little armour their chieftains do appear to have used more extensive lamellar defences than the more limited armours of the western steppes. This may have reflected a continuing tradition in northern China and the eastern steppes. Here a leader has a cuirass and arm-pieces in which alternate rows of lamellae are covered with decorative fabric. His iron segmented helmet is sturdy but simple while his chisel-ended sabre is of a form that spread from the steppes to the Muslim world even before the rise of the Mongols. (Main sources: based on a reconstruction by M. V. Gorelik, plus early Mongol weapons and harness fittings, ex-Pletnyeva.)

K2: Naiman warrior, 12th century

The Naiman were Mongols but were more advanced than their eastern cousins. This man is a Nestorian Christian and his armour of large scales fastened to a leather base has much in common with earlier forms of European coats-of-plates. His single-edged spear is a cutting as well as thrusting weapon. (Main sources: Kirghiz sword, 10th–12th C., ex-Khudyakov; spearhead, 11th–12th C., ex-Khudyakov; scale armour and helmet, 12th–13th C., ex-Khudyakov; Christian cross from northern Caucasus, 10th–11th C., ex-Pletnyeva.)

K3: Karakhitai nobleman, 11th–12th centuries

No surviving illustrations seem to portray specifically Karakhitai warriors but others do illustrate Uighurs at a time when they were ruled by the Karakhitai and the two peoples are likely to have been very similar. This horseman is dressed and equipped in a very elaborate form of eastern steppe style with a great deal of Chinese influence. This

Life-like carvings were also made in Muslim Turkish Daghestan, in the Caucasus. This shows a typical Central Asian horse-archer using the rearwards 'Parthian Shot'. He carries a large box-like quiver, a composite bow and stirrups. (Hermitage Mus., Leningrad)

influence is most obvious in the long-hafted glaive that he carries. Such unlikely cavalry weapons continued to be seen in Central Asian sources into the 15th century and were probably spread as a result of the Mongol conquests. (Source: 'Uighurs pay homage to Guo Zui', Chinese scroll painting, 11th–12th C., Nat. Palace Mus., Taipei.)

L: The western steppes, 10th–13th centuries
L1: Volga Bulgar cavalryman, 12th–early 13th centuries

Excavated arms, armour and harness from the Volga Bulgar region suggest that they were similar to their Russian rivals. This man has a distinctive form of segmented helmet with a large nasal and half-visor normally associated with Russia but also illustrated in western Siberia. He is otherwise protected by a short mail hauberk which is longer at the front than the back, plus a piece of lamellar armour over his chest. His silver-inlaid war-axe is specifically Volga Bulgar while his sabre is of the ring-pommel type. From his belt are suspension hooks for a quiver and bowcase. (Main sources: miniature helmet, possibly harness decoration, west Siberian, 10th–12th C., ex-Solovyev; war-axe, Volga Bulgar, 12th–13th C., ex-Pletnyeva; mail shirt from Kiev region, nomad 'Black Hat', 12th–13th C., Hist. Mus., Zitomirsk.)

L2: Kipchaq warrior, 12th century

The Kipchaqs were one of the last of the western steppe nomads to leave a great deal of weaponry in their graves and to make funerary statues. Their most characteristic piece of equipment was a tall pointed helmet with an anthropomorphic iron or bronze visor. Their cavalry elite also wore short-sleeved mail hauberks, a small amount of lamellar armour and fought with bows and curved sabres. (Main sources: helmet and mail hauberk from Kovali, Kipchaq or early Mongol, 12th–13th C., State Hist. Mus., Moscow; stone funeral statues from Dnepr region, 11th–12th C., ex-Pletnyeva; belt, sword, bowcase, whip and harness pieces from western steppes, 11th–13th C., ex-Pletnyeva.)

L3: Pecheneg lady, 10th–11th century

The female costume of the nomads is easier to reconstruct than that of the forest peoples. Although both buried their dead with jewellery and various female work tools, such as the scissors and fire-striker hanging from this woman's belt, the nomads also made lifelike stone statues to be placed over their graves. From these we can tell that some Pecheneg women wore tall hats, perhaps of felt, decorated tunics and riding boots similar to those worn by their menfolk. (Main sources: jewellery and other grave goods from the western steppes, 11th–12th C., ex-Pletnyeva; stone funerary statues from the Dnepr and neighbouring regions, 11th–13th C., ex-Pletnyeva.)

Notes sur les planches en couleur

A1 Armure à lamelles de bronze sur la tête, le cou et les jambes et de cuir sur le corps. **A2** Grand bouclier rectangulaire, porté souvent sur le dos, caractéristique de l'art Tashtyk. **A3** L'on peut voir un mélange d'influences indienne (pour la coiffure de tête), chinoise (épée) et de l'est de l'Iran (vêtements).

B1 Costume Hun principalement; l'étui d'arc contient deux arcs sans corde, et il porte un arc garni d'or, symbole de son autorité. Epée et fourreau en or, jade et lapis lazuli d'une qualité princière, de même que le harnachement et la selle. **B2** Le casque et l'épée sont des Sarmates ou des Alains, le reste du costume est germanique. **B3** Bien que parlant le grec, les natifs du Bosphore subirent l'influence des nomades avant l'arrivée des Huns. Le casque segmenté est retenu par des lanières de cuir; la cuirasse à lamelles de fer est l'écho des styles romains de fin de période, et le fourreau est germanique.

C1 L'art Toba montre des styles de costume du centre de l'Asie, quoique probablement de matériaux chinois; le manteau présente une influence *Sughdienne*; le poignard est du nord de la Chine et l'épée chinoise de style. **C2** L'armure est faite en cuir principalement, notez les pièces d'épaule amovibles. Les protections de cou au rembourrage épais sont caractéristiques de cette période ancienne. Notez les étriers. **C3** Armure pour le corps en peaux superposées; notez les vastes boucliers de l'infanterie de Chine septentrionale sous domination *Toba*, que l'on vit également en Asie centrale et qui furent probablement utilisés par les Huns.

D1 Magnifique noble *Transoxanian* pré-Islam; de style iranien bien qu'il ait conservé le style nomadique de coiffure à nattes. **D2** D'après des peintures murales de *Piandjikent*; notez le casque en fer et cuir, le cotte de mailles, l'étui à crayons et la bourse sur la ceinture avec la dague et la masse d'armes en bronze. **D3** Guerrier de l'élite de cette région qui est devenue l'Afghanistan, un mélange des modes asiatique et iranienne; haubert en mailles sous la tunique serrée, et guêtres de cuir décorées.

E1 Notez la ceinture à breloque de l'élite d'Asie centrale, le long carquois, et deux arcs, l'un porté sans corde dans un étui à charnière; épée à pommeau à anneau et casque d'Europe centrale qui a été pris à l'ennemi. La selle, avec étriers, à une monture en bois que remplace la forme rembourrée primitive. **E2** La tunique et les pantalons font apparaître l'influence byzantine; le casque est un *spangenhelm* à monture de fer simple. **E3** Uniforme ex-byzantin en loques, casque germanique, hache et javelots slaves.

F1 D'après les peintures murales de Piandjikent, un héros magnifiquement paré dans une lourde armure de Transoxiane, les manches "tête de lion" rappelant des descriptions du héros médiéval persan Rustam par les poètes. **F2** Des plumes doubles sur le casque identifiant l'archer à cheval champion; notez les petites clochettes sur la lance – populaires parmi les guerriers turcs – et l'armure à lamelles, celle de la cuirasse couverte de bandes de tissu tandis que l'armure du cheval ne l'est pas. **F3** Il tire du sang du cou de son cheval comme ration d'urgence, porte le costume typique de la steppe, bien que la longue chevelure soit typiquement turque. De simples étriers à boucle de cuir furent utilisés par les guerriers plus pauvres jusqu'en vers la fin du 14ème siècle.

G1 La garniture de tête pourrait bien avoir été une indication de rang. Les Timurides musulmans portaient encore la ceinture large en tissu sous leur ceinturon, au 15ème siècle. L'étui de l'arc et le carquois ont des formes médiévales entièrement développées. Les bottes lacées sur une ceinture non visible rappellent des modes plus anciennes. **G2** Casque en lamelles de bronze sur une base épaisse de cuir rembourré; l'armure du corps en cuir durci, certaines sections étant laquées. **G3** L'on rencontrait fréquemment des marchands *Sughdiens*, sur la Grande Route de la Soie, ce commerçant avec un

Farbtafeln

A1 Lamellenpanzer aus Bronze auf Kopf, Hals und Beinen, Leder am Körper. **A2** Großer rechteckiger Schild, oft am Rücken getragen, typisch für Tashtyk-Kunst. **A3** Sichtbare Einflüsse sind: Mischung aus Indisch (Kopfbedeckung), Chinesisch (Schwert) und Ostpersisch (Kleidung).

B1 Grundlegende Hunnenkleidung; der Bogenbehälter enthält zwei Bogen ohne Sehnen, und er trägt einen goldenen Bogen als Symbol de Authorität. Schwert aus Gold, jade und Lapislazuli samt Scheide sind von fürstlicher Qualität, ebenso das Sattelzeug. **B2** Helm und Schwert stammen von Sarmaten oder Alanen, restliches Kostüm germanisch. **B3** Die Bosphoros-Leute sprachen zwar Griechisch, waren aber vor Ankunft der Hunnen von Nomaden beeinflußt. Der abteilige Helm wird von Lederriemen zusammengehalten; der eiserne Lamellen-panzer erinnert an spätrömische Vorbilder, die Scheide ist germanisch.

C1 Toba-Kunst zeigt zentralasiatische Kostüme, aber wahrscheinlich aus chinesischen Materialien; der Mantel zeigt sughdischen Einfluß; der Dolch stammt aus Nordchina, das Schwert zeigt klaren chinesischen Stil. **C2** Panzer hauptsächlich aus gehärtetem Leder, siehe abnehmbare Schulterstücke. Stark gepolsterte Halsteile sind für diese frühe Periode typisch. Siehe Steigbügel. **C3** Panzer aus sich überschneidenden Rindslederteilen: siehe große Schilde der nordchinesischen Infanterie unter Toba-Herrschaft, wie man sie auch in Zentralasien findet und wie sie vielleicht von den Hunnen verwendet wurden.

D2 Aus den Piandjikent-Wandmalerein; siehe den Eisen- und Lederhelm, Panzerhemd, Federkasten und Börse am Gürtel, mit Bronze-Streitkolben. **D1** Vornehmer, vorislamischer transoxanischer Edelmann; iranischer Stil, aber Nomadenzöpfe beibehalten. **D3** Elitekrieger aus der Gegend des heutigen Afghanistan, in gemischter zentralasiatischer und iranischer Mode; eiserner Halskragen unter enger Tunika, verzierte Lederhosent räger.

E1 Siehe Gürtel der zentralasiatischen Elite, langen Köcher und zwei Bogen, einer sehnenlos in Scharnierbehälter; Schwert unde erbeuteter mitteleuropäischer helm. Sattel mit Steigbügeln hat einen Holzrahmen, nicht die primitivere, gepolsterte Art. **E2** Tunika und Hose zeigen byzantinischen Einfluß; der Helm ist ein simpler Spangenhelm aus Leder mit Eisenrahmen. **E3** Zerlumpte ehemalige byzantinische Uniform, germanischer Helm, slawische Axt und Speer.

F1 Aus Piandjikent-Wandmalereien, ein großartig ausgestatteter Mann in Schwerem transsylvanischen Panzer mit "Löwenkopf"-Ärmeln, die an poetische Schilderungen des mittelalterlichen persischen Helden Rustam erinnern. **F2** Zwei Federn am Helm identifizieren einen berittenen Champion-Bogenschützen; siehe Glöckchen am Speer – beliebt bei türkischen Kriegern – und Leder-Lamellenpanzer, am Küraß mit Stoffstreifen bedeckt, nicht aber der Pferdepanzer. **F3** Er zapft vom hals seines Pferdes Blut als Notration ab und trägt typische Steppenkleidung, obwohl sein langes Haar rein Tükisch ist. Einfache Schlingen-Steigbügel aus Leder wurden von den ärmeren Soldaten bis weit ins 14. Jahrhundert getragen.

G1 Die Kopfbedeckung dürfte wohl ein Rangabzeichen sein. Die breite Schärpe unter dem Gürtel wurde von den moslemischen Timuriden im 15. Jahrhundert noch getragen. Bogenbehälter und Köcher sind vollentwickelte mittelalterliche Formen. Die Stiefel, mit einem unsichtbaren Gürel verschnürt, erinnern an ältere Vorbilder. **G2** Helm aus Bronze auf dicker Lederpolsterung; Panzer aus gehärtetem Leder, teilweise lackiert. **G3** Auf der großen "Seidenstraße" waren sughdische Kaufleute oft zu finden, wie dieser Händler in Pferdepanzervierzierungen, in sughdischer Mode mit zentralasiatischeen Zugaben für die winterliche Kälte; de Säbel ist persische, der Gürtel türkisch.

harnaise de cheval décoré porte les modes *Sughdiennes* avec des additions d'Asie centrale contre le froid de l'hiver; le sabre est iranian, la ceinture turque.

H1 Ce costume presque complet d'un noble Alain a été retrouvé dans une tombe du nord du Caucase. Notez la parure de tête doublée de cuir avec épi métallique; *kaftan* islamique iranien; sabre incurvé; étui d'arc simple en cuir; et dague élégante argentée. **H2** Casque de fer forgé d'une seule pièce, haubert en mailles long et défenses de membres à éclisses, semblables aux premiers modèles scandinaves. Seul le sabre présente une influence turque de la steppe. **H3** Les styles irano-islamiques sont décrits dans des manuscrits et cet homme a un casque de fer couvert de cuivre avec un long ventail de mailles. Notez la cuirasse à lamelles de fer sur la cotte de mailles à manches longues; et la lame de l'épée arabe à la poignée de style arménien en bronze.

I1 Bien qu'ils furent isolés, les Kirghiz avaient des formes élaborées de parure de guerre – notez le beau casque. Des lames superposées de fer protègent la poitrine, sur un manteau en pourpoint. L'épée reste droite à double tranchant. **I2** L'on a retrouvé de nombreuses armures à lamelles et à écailles dans les tombes de Kimak. Le casque segmenté est caractéristique des steppes et de la Russie médiévale. **I3** L'équipement des Kirghiz d'une date plus récente présente une influence chinoise, il en est de même du costume mongol d'une date plus avancée. L'on peut voir sur ce soldat, qui est protégé principalement par des lamelles de fer, le début d'une armure à plates – notez les pièces d'épaule, de poitrine et de genou.

J1 Les articles disposés dans les tombes font également état d'une grande richesse parmi l'élite des peuplades de la forêt septentrionale. **J2** Les tombes des hommes ne sont pas aussi riches en général; le guerrier est armé d'une lance, d'un javelot léger et d'une hache de jet. Le casque a été retrouvé en Prusse balte mais est un modèle courant de la région septentrionale. **J3** Cuirasse de peaux à lamelles sous un lourd manteau de fourrure; sabre caractéristique des steppes centrales et de la Sibérie sous la selle; et large sabre, apparemment un article d'échange venu de l'Ouest.

K1 Cuirasse à lamelles décorative et défenses de bras, présentant une influence du nord de la Chine/de la région des steppes à l'est, et simple casque à segments en fer. **K2** Bien que ce guerrier chrétien nestorien soit mongol, sa parure est plus élaborée que celle de ses cousins de la région Est – armure en écailles larges sur une base de cuir, lance à un tranchant pour couper/jeter et une hache avec marteau au revers. **K3** Reconstitution spéculative d'après des sources d'époque d'Uighur à une date où les Uighurs étaient sous la domination de Karakhitai. Costume élaboré de la région Est des steppes présentant une influence chinoise; notez le glaie à manche long peu commun, vue sur des sources d'Asie centrale jusqu'au 15ème siècle.

L1 Costume remis au jour lors d'excavations dans la région de la Volga Bulgar qui suggère des similarités avec les styles russes d'époque. Le casque au large nasal et à la demi-visière est russe ou de la région Ouest de la Sibérie; la hache aux incrustations d'argent est de la Volga Bulgar; les anneaux sur la ceinture peuvent supporter un carquois et un étui à arc; notez également le haubert qui est plus long devant que derrière, avec une pièce de poitrine à lamelles. **L2** Les riches objets déposés dans les tombes ont permis de faire une reconstitution de ce Kipchaq, au haut casque pointu complet avec sa visière anthropomorphique; haubert à manches courtes et une petite quantité d'armure à lamelles; un arc et un sabre incurvé. **L3** A nouveau les riches pieces déposées et la statuaire des tombes ont permis cette reconstitution avec une assez grande confiance.

H1 Das fast komplette Kostüm eines alanischen Edlen wurde in einem Gr nördlichen Kaukasus gefunden. Siehe lederbesetzte Kopfbedeckung mit persischen Kaftanmantel. Krummsäbel, einfachen ledernen Bogenbehälte schönen Silberdolch. **H2** Einteiliger Schmiedeeisen-Helm, Panzer-Hals und Gliederschutz, ähnlich frühen skandinavischen Vorbildern. Nur de erinnert an türkische Steppeneinflüsse. **H3** Iranisch-islamische Stilrichtu werden in schriftlichen berichten beschrieben, und dieser Mann trägt Kupferbedeckten Eisenhelm mit langem Panzer-Aventail. Siehe eis Lamellenpanzer über langärmeligem Panzerhemd, und arabische Sch klinge mit armenischem Bronzegriff.

I1 Die isolierten Kirgisen hatten doch modernes Kriegsgerät – sieh schönen Helm. Überhängende Eisenlamellen schützen die Brust über gesteppten mantel. Das Schwert ist immer noch von der geraden, zweisch gen Art. **I2** Kimak-Gräber enthalternn Panzer, die ein Mittelding zwi Lamellen- und Schuppenpanzern sind. Der mehrteilige Helm ist typisch f mittelalterlichen Steppen und Rußland. **I3** Spätere kirgisische Ausrüstung chinesischen Einfluß, aber auch Ähnlichkeit mit späten mongolischen S Hauptsächlich durch Eisenlamellen geschützt, zeigt dieser Mann den d chen beginn des Plattenpanzers – siehe Schulter-, Brust- und Kniestücke.

J1 Grabinhalte zeigen großen Reichtum unter der Elite der nördl Waldvölker. **J2** Männergräber sind meist nicht so reich; der Krieger hier i einem typisch finnischen Messer, einem Speer, ener Lanze und einer W bewaffnet. Der Helm wurde im baltischen Preußen gefunden, ist abe allgemein nördlicher Art. **J3** Rindsleder-Lamellenpanzer unter schw Pelzmantel; der Säbel ist typisch für die zentralen Steppen und Sibirien, dem Sattel; und ein Pallasch, offenbar im Westen erworben.

K1 Verzierter lamellenpanzer mit Armschutz zeigt nordchines Steppeneinfluß; simpler mehrteiliger Eisenhelm. **K2** Obwohl ein Mor verfügt dieser christliche Krieget über modernere Ausrüstung als östl Vettern – Panzer mit großen Schuppen auf Leder, einen einschneidigen Wurfspeer und eine Axt mit Hammerseite. **K3** Spekulative Rekonstrui aus zeitgenössischen Uighurenquellen, als die Uighuren von Kara beherrscht wurden. Komplexes Kostüm aus den östlichen Steppenmit chi chem Einfluß; siehe unübliches Schwert mit langen Griff, wie man zentralasiatischen Quellen bis ins 15. Jahrhundert hinein findet.

L1 Aus der bulgarischen Wolgagegend ausgegrabene Geräte lassen Äh keiten mit zeitgenössischen russischen Stilrichtungen erkennen. Der Heli großem Nasenschützer und Halbvisier ist russisch oder westsibirisch; di Silber eingelegt Axt bulgarisch; Haken am Gürtel sind für Köcher Bogenbehälter bestimmt; siehe Halsberge die vorne länger als hinten i Lamellen-Brustschutz. **L2** Reiche Grabfunde ermöglichen die Nachbi dieses Kipchaq, mit hohem, spitzen Helm mit gesichtsförmigem V kurzärmelige Halsberge und wenig Lamellenpanzer; Bogen und Krumm **L3** Wiederum ermöglichen reiche Grabfunde und Statuen eine recht zuve tliche Rekonstruktion.